Little Hands
to Heaven

A Preschool Program for Ages 2-5

Written by Carrie Austin, M.Ed.

Editor:

Julie Grosz

Cover Designer:

Merlin DeBoer

Heart of Dakota Publishing
www.heartofdakota.com

Special Thanks to:

- Julie Grosz for her patient editing, kind words, continuous support, and willingness to pilot this program with her own children.

- Cindy Madden for her helpful ideas and her willingness to pilot this program with her own children.

- Mike Austin for his unwavering support and love, positive attitude, and consistent willingness to do whatever is needed. Without him, there would be no *Little Hands to Heaven.*

- Christian Store for posing as a live model for the cover of the book and truly showing his little hands raised to heaven.

Copyright 2003, 2007, 2010 by Carrie Austin
Heart of Dakota Publishing, Inc.
1004 Westview Drive
Dell Rapids, SD 57022

Website: www.heartofdakota.com
Phone (605) 428-4068

Printed in the U.S.A.

ISBN 0-9747695-4-1

Table of Contents

Introduction

Educational

Little Hands to Heaven is a complete preschool program that includes letter recognition and formation, letter sounds with corresponding motions, beginning math skills, Bible activities, devotional topics, art projects, dramatic play, active exploration, fingerplays, and music.

Bible-based

Little Hands to Heaven is a collection of 33 units based on stories from the Bible. Each unit has a theme centered around Bible characters. The activities in each unit coordinate with the daily Bible stories.

Easy to Use

Each unit contains 5 days of instruction. Simple daily plans have the work already done for you. Quick and easy activities require little or no preparation and use only materials you're likely to have on hand. There is no literature to gather. Simply use your Bible or purchase one of the listed Bible storybooks, and you are set for the whole program.

Fun Activities

Engaging daily lessons take approximately 30 minutes or less. They are filled with ideas that get kids moving, exploring, and playing in a meaningful way.

Flexible

Activities are not seasonal or holiday related, which allows you to make the program fit your schedule. Lesson plans are written so you can use the program with students of multiple ages at the same time. A choice of resources is provided for the Bible stories and devotions, so you have the option of selecting what best suits your needs.

Resources

Choose one of the following Bibles to use with this program:
A Child's First Bible by Kenneth N. Taylor (Tyndale House, 2000),
The New Bible in Pictures for Little Eyes by Kenneth N. Taylor (Moody, 2002), or your own personal Bible.

Choose one of the following devotionals to use with this program:
Big Thoughts for Little People by Kenneth N. Taylor (Tyndale Kids, 2009),
Teach Them to Your Children: An Alphabet of Biblical Poems, Verses, and Stories (The Vision Forum, Inc., 2006), or *My ABC Bible Verses* by Susan Hunt (Crossway, 1998) Musical selections from Focus on the Family's *The Singing Bible* (Tyndale House, 2007) correspond with each unit and are included in the daily plans.

Program Components

Bible Story

Each unit has a theme centered around Bible characters. The themes are organized in chronological order from creation through Paul's missionary journeys. Bible stories related to the theme are read aloud each day. These stories provide the focus for the day's plans. The daily activities are linked to the Bible stories.

Fingerplay

A new fingerplay is introduced each unit. Each fingerplay emphasizes one letter and its sound, while also reinforcing the Biblical theme. Every 5th unit is a letter review unit.

Letter Activity

Daily letter activities emphasize the same letter and letter sound as the fingerplay. Each unit includes each of the following letter activities:

* letter flashcards with corresponding sounds and motions
* letter art which increases awareness of the letter shapes
* letter action with whole body movement to trace masking tape letters
* letter slide which provides tactile activities for each letter
* letter hide and seek with practice in finding a letter in context and in matching uppercase and lowercase letters

Bible Activity

A variety of daily Bible activities teach skills such as number and color recognition, counting, cutting, gluing, coloring, listening skills, directional words, dramatization, and life application.

Corresponding Music

Musical selections from Focus on the Family's *The Singing Bible* correspond with each unit. The original songs retell the Bible stories using a variety of musical styles.

Art Activity

One day in each unit includes an art activity that reinforces the Biblical theme. In order to encourage self-expression, the creative activities focus on the artistic process rather than the product.

Active Exploration

One day in each unit includes active exploration based on the Biblical theme. Hands on, concrete experiences help children make connections to the world around them.

Devotional Activity

One day in each unit includes a devotional activity that supports the Biblical theme. A related story or fingerplay, corresponding Scripture verse, and a prayer are part of each devotion.

Dramatic Play

One day in each unit includes dramatic play that reinforces the Biblical theme. Dramatizations based on the Bible story encourage creativity, using play to learn skills.

Math Activity

One day in each unit includes a math activity. These activities gently introduce mathematical concepts through guided play. The activities reinforce the Biblical theme. A brief scope and sequence of the math concepts is listed by unit below (Number '1' corresponds to unit 1, number '2' corresponds to unit 2, etc.):

1 - patterns and colors
2 - patterns and counting
3 - sequencing letters and numbers (names and phone numbers)
4 - general measurement: comparing distances
5 - money: coin recognition
6 - counting steps
7 - comparing: few/many, once/more than once, tall/short
8 - ordinal numbers: first, second, third
9 - counting to 10: one to one correspondance
10 - patterns, shapes, counting
11 - general weight measurement: light/heavy
12 - auditory patterns
13 - comparing sizes: smallest/largest
14 - general length measurement: ordering longest to shortest
15 - matching and ordering by size: smallest to largest
16 - sorting and classifying
17 - counting, early addition/subtraction, zero
18 - counting, spatial terms, inside/outside
19 - duplicating patterns, spatial terms: away from
20 - counting and making sets
21 - tracing or copying designs and finding shapes
22 - counting: one to one correspondance
23 - comparing numbers: more than/less than/equal to
24 - counting and addition combinations that equal 5
25 - general measurement: area
26 - nonstandard measurement: "feet"
27 - sorting, counting, and graphing sets
28 - money: coin recognition, value, counting
29 - general time: yesterday, today, tomorrow
30 - number sense: more than 1 and counting forward/backward
31 - counting forward/backward and early addition
32 - general fractions: whole vs. part
33 - sorting and classifying: color, size, and shape

Fine Motor- Kumon Mazes & cutting
Read Tops & Bottoms - weefolkart.com
Berenstain Almanac - pg 4-7

Math LHFHG
The Reading Lesson

Creation and the Fall

Fingerplay

Do the fingerplay *"Adam and the Animals"*. Focus on the sound and motion for the letter 'A'.

Key Idea: 'A' = place hands on cheeks, act surprised, and say *A-A*

Letter Activity

Copy the 'A' flashcard found in the Appendix. Show the letter side of the flashcard to the students. Read the *Hint* aloud. Demonstrate the motion and sound for 'A'. Have the students repeat it.

Key Idea: Students should eventually do the motion and say the sound for each flashcard without needing a *Hint* or a demonstration from you.

Bible Story

Read the Bible story from **one** of the following resources:

✔ Scripture: Genesis 1:1-5
✔ *A Child's First Bible* p. 6-7
✔ *The New Bible in Pictures for Little Eyes* p. 14-15

Key Idea: God made the world.

Bible Activity

Turn off the light and have students cover their eyes. Say, *See how dark it was before God created everything. There was nothing. God said, "Let there be light..."*

Have students uncover their eyes. Turn on the lights. Have students point and name objects they see.

Key Idea: God created everything. Without him, there would be nothing.

Art Activity

Tell students to draw objects or marks on **white paper** with **white crayons**. Possible ideas for objects include stars, moon, trees, sun, animals, planets, and people.

Use water to **dilute black tempera paint**. Have students paint over the drawings to make them appear.

Key Idea: God created all things from nothing. Could you do that?

Corresponding Music

The Singing Bible, Disc 1 - Track 3
Song Title: "*God Made the Universe*

Fingerplay: Adam and the Animals

Days 1-5

A-A-Adam!	*Hands on cheeks in surprise*
Can you believe?	*Hands out, palms up*
God made animals	*Point out sweeping arm across*
And you and me?	*Point out and then to yourself*
A-A-Adam!	*Hands on cheeks in surprise*
Can you believe?	*Hands out, palms up*
God made ants	*Lightly walk on all fours*
To crawl, you see?	
A-A-Adam!	*Hands on cheeks in surprise*
Can you believe?	*Hands out, palms up*
God made alligators	*Slide on belly, using arms and*
To slide, you see?	*legs to push along floor*
A-A-Adam!	*Hands on cheeks in surprise*
Can you believe?	*Hands out, palms up*
God made antelope	*Leap in the air*
To leap, you see?	
A-A-Adam!	*Hands on cheeks in surprise*
Can you believe?	*Hands out, palms up*
God made anteaters	*On all fours, slide nose along*
To sniff, you see?	*close to the ground*
A-A-Adam!	*Hands on cheeks in surprise*
Can you believe?	*Hands out, palms up*
God made the albatross	*Flap arms like wings*
To fly, you see?	*Fly around the room*
A-A-Adam!	*Hands on cheeks in surprise*
Can you believe?	*Hands out, palms up*
God made anacondas	*Slide on belly with arms above*
To slither, you see?	*head*

Creation and the Fall

Fingerplay

Do the fingerplay *"Adam and the Animals"*. Focus on the sound and motion for the letter 'A'.

<u>Key Idea:</u> 'A' = place hands on cheeks, act surprised, and say *A-A*

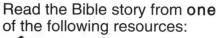

Bible Story

Read the Bible story from **one** of the following resources:

✔ Scripture: Genesis 2:1

✔ *A Child's First Bible* p. 6-7

✔ *The New Bible in Pictures for Little Eyes* p. 16-17

<u>Key Idea:</u> God created all things.

Math Activity

<u>Youngers:</u> Choose several colors to emphasize. Students make a circle with a crayon on a piece of paper for each chosen color. Have students take a walk with the paper and look for those colors in their surroundings.
<u>Olders:</u> Have students check their surroundings for patterns such as polka dots, swirls, florals, checks and plaids. Students may draw the patterns.

<u>Key Idea:</u> God created all the colors and patterns that we see.

Letter Activity

Use masking tape to make a large 'A' on the floor. Have students walk a stuffed animal on the tape to trace the letter. Then, have students walk the letter themselves, saying the letter **sound** as they walk.

<u>Key Idea:</u> Each letter has a name and a sound, just like animals do.
For example, a cat may be named Fluffy, but it makes the sound, *Meow.*

Bible Activity

Copy *Count on Me* (in Appendix). Direct students to draw caterpillars by making a green squiggle in the boxes. Younger students make 1 caterpillar in each box. Older students make 2 caterpillars in each box. Point to each caterpillar as you count it with the students. Write the numbers on the lines below each box as you count. Say the numbers below the boxes to count by 1's or by 2's (counting either '1', '2', '3' ... or '2', '4', '6' ...).

<u>Key Idea:</u> God made each animal very special.

Corresponding Music

The Singing Bible, Disc 1 - Track 3
Song Title: *"God Made the Universe"*

Creation and the Fall

Unit 1 - Day 3

Fingerplay

Do the fingerplay *"Adam and the Animals"*. Focus on the sound and motion for the letter 'A'.

Key Idea: 'A' = place hands on cheeks, act surprised, and say *A-A*

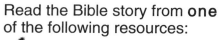

Bible Story

Read the Bible story from **one** of the following resources:

✔ Scripture: Genesis 1:26-27; 2:7

✔ *A Child's First Bible* p. 8-9

✔ *The New Bible in Pictures for Little Eyes* p. 18-19

Key Idea: God made people.

Devotional Activity

Read and discuss the devotion from **one** of the following resources:

✔ *Big Thoughts for Little People*
Read the two pages for letter 'A'.

✔ *Teach Them to Your Children*
Read the two pages for letter 'A'.

✔ *My ABC Bible Verses*
Read the two pages for letter 'A'.

Key Idea: Share a devotional focusing on character traits or memory work based on the letter 'A'.

Letter Activity

Write a big 'A' on a piece of paper. Have students glue dry 'O'-shaped cereal or dried beans to the letter. Younger students will need you to apply drops of glue on the letter for them first.

Key Idea: Students will become familiar with the shape and appearance of the capital letter 'A'.

Bible Activity

Act out the Bible story. Give students the following list of directions: *Pretend to pick up dust and blow breath into it as God did. Outline a person in the air and say, "Adam". Lay Adam down to sleep and pretend to take a rib out for Eve. Outline Eve in the air and say, "Eve". Point to yourself and say your own name. Lift your arms to heaven and say, "Thank you God for making me."*

Key Idea: God created you in his image.

Corresponding Music

The Singing Bible, Disc 1 - Track 3
Song Title: *"God Made the Universe"*

~ pg 9-10
renstain - pg 16-19 ✻
s & Bottoms
+ Dough Veggies

Creation and the Fall

Fingerplay

Do the fingerplay *"Adam and the Animals"*. Focus on the sound and motion for the letter 'A'.

<u>Key Idea</u>: 'A' = place hands on cheeks, act surprised, and say *A-A*

Letter Activity

Copy the *Hide and Seek 'A'* page. Have students circle, color, highlight, or point to the 'A's on the page. Younger students may need help in order to find any 'A's at all. It is not necessary to find all the 'A's. On the bottom of the page, have students connect 'A' to 'a' by tracing the dotted line from left to right.

<u>Key Idea</u>: Students should eventually recognize the capital and small letter 'A' within words.

Bible Story

Read the Bible story from **one** of the following resources:

✔ Scripture: Genesis 3:2-6
✔ *A Child's First Bible* p. 10-11
✔ *The New Bible in Pictures for Little Eyes* p. 20-21

<u>Key Idea</u>: Adam and Eve disobeyed.

Bible Activity

Copy the *Number One* page. Have students find one tree in a magazine or catalog to cut out. Use a marker to circle, box, or outline the tree so that students have a line to follow as they cut. Have students glue the tree on the *Number One* page. Save this page. A page will be added each week to make a '1-10' counting book.

<u>Key Idea</u>: God sent Adam and Eve out of the Garden of Eden because they disobeyed him. How do you think God feels when you disobey?

Dramatic Play

Lay a scarf, jump rope, or long belt on the floor in a straight line. Pretend it is a snake. Have students practice jumping with their feet together over the snake. Students can jump forward, backward, and sideways. Next, wiggle the snake close to the ground telling students to jump over or away from it.

<u>Key Idea</u>: Adam and Eve should have stayed away from the snake.

Corresponding Music

The Singing Bible, Disc 1 – Tracks 4, 5
Song Titles: *"Two Trees"*
           "God's Promise"

Hide and Seek 'A'

A-A-Adam!

Can you believe?

God made animals

And you and me?

Number
One

1

Creation and the Fall

Unit 1 - Day 5

Fingerplay

Do the fingerplay *"Adam and the Animals"*. Focus on the sound and motion for the letter 'A'.

Key Idea: 'A' = place hands on cheeks, act surprised, and say *A-A*

Letter Activity

Use the 'A' flashcard from the Appendix. Have students trace the capital and small letter 'A's' on the flashcard with their fingers. Using the flashcard as a model, choose either a bar of soap on a mirror or an ice cube on construction paper to have students write more 'A's'.

Key Idea: Practice the motions needed to make the letter 'A'.

Bible Story

Read the Bible story from **one** of the following resources:

✔ Scripture: Genesis 4:3-10

✔ *A Child's First Bible* p. 12-13

✔ *The New Bible in Pictures for Little Eyes* p. 22-23

Key Idea: Cain killed Abel.

Bible Activity

Have students make mad faces, hit their stuffed animals, throw them on the ground, and walk away. Have students pick up their animals and say instead, *Please don't do that! It makes me upset. Let's get along.* Tell students to shake hands with their stuffed animal and twirl around. Ask, *Which of these two ways does God want us to act when we are mad? What are some things that make you angry?*

Key Idea: Cain should not have hurt Abel, even though he was mad at him. God says to love others.

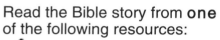

Active Exploration

People show how they feel with their faces, words, and voices. Have students make a matching face as they say each of the following phrases: *I'm angry. I'm so sleepy. I'm really sad. I am so excited!* Tell students to sing *"Row, Row, Row Your Boat"* using different voices to express each of the emotions listed above. You may want to add hand gestures or have students look in a mirror.

Key Idea: Cain's anger got him into trouble because he killed Abel.

Corresponding Music

The Singing Bible, Disc 1 – Track 6
Song Title: *"Cain and Abel"*

renstain pg 20-21
mon Mazes & cut
ad Beatrice's Goat

The Earth and the Flood

Fingerplay

Do the fingerplay *"Noah's Big Boat"*. Focus on the sound and motion for the letter 'B'.

Key Idea: 'B' = hug yourself, rock side to side, and say *B-B*

Letter Activity

Copy the 'B' flashcard found in the Appendix. Show the letter side of the flashcard to the students. Read the *Hint* aloud. Demonstrate the motion and sound for 'B'. Have the students repeat it. Review the flashcards from previous weeks.

Key Idea: Students should eventually do the motion and say the sound for each flashcard without needing a *Hint* or a demonstration from you.

Bible Story

Read the Bible story from **one** of the following resources:

✔ Scripture: Genesis 6:9-14, 18-19

✔ *A Child's First Bible* p. 14-15

✔ *The New Bible in Pictures for Little Eyes* p. 24-25

Key Idea: Noah built a boat.

Bible Activity

Copy the *Number Two* page. Have students find two hands in a magazine or catalog to cut out. Use a marker to circle, box, or outline each hand so that students have a line to follow as they cut. Have students glue the hands on the *Number Two* page. Save this page. A page will be added each week to make a '1-10' counting book.

Key Idea: Noah used his hands to do what God told him to do. He built the ark exactly as God said.

Devotional Activity

Read and discuss the devotion from **one** of the following resources:

✔ *Big Thoughts for Little People*
Read the two pages for letter 'B'.

✔ *Teach Them to Your Children*
Read the two pages for letter 'B'.

✔ *My ABC Bible Verses*
Read the two pages for letter 'B'.

Key Idea: Share a devotional focusing on character traits or memory work based on the letter 'B'.

Corresponding Music

The Singing Bible, Disc 1 - Track 7
Song Title: *"Noah Build a Boat"*

Fingerplay: Noah's Big Boat

Days 1-5

Two big bears got on the boat.   *Hold up two fingers*
The rains came down,   *Fingers flutter down*
And the boat did float.   *Run fingers back and forth*
B... B... B...   *Hug yourself and rock side-to-side*
The animals played and played,   *Point fingers up on head like ears*
And Noah heard the big bears say,   *Cup hand around ear*
Grrr! Grrr! Grrr!   *Cup hands around mouth*

Two baboons got on the boat.   *Hold up two fingers*
The rains came down,   *Fingers flutter down*
And the boat did float.   *Run fingers back and forth*
B... B... B...   *Hug yourself and rock side-to-side*
The animals played and played,   *Point fingers up on head like ears*
And Noah heard the baboons say,   *Cup hand around ear*
Ooh! Ooh! Ooh!   *Cup hands around mouth*

Two bald eagles got on the boat.   *Hold up two fingers*
The rains came down,   *Fingers flutter down*
And the boat did float.   *Run fingers back and forth*
B... B... B...   *Hug yourself and rock side-to-side*
The animals played and played,   *Point fingers up on head like ears*
And Noah heard the eagles say,   *Cup hand around ear*
Eeh! Eeh! Eeh!   *Cup hands around mouth*

Two brown beavers got on the boat.   *Hold up two fingers*
The rains came down,   *Fingers flutter down*
And the boat did float.   *Run fingers back and forth*
B... B... B...   *Hug yourself and rock side-to-side*
The animals played and played,   *Point fingers up on head like ears*
And Noah heard the beavers say,   *Cup hand around ear*
Chomp! Chomp! Chomp!   *Cup hands around mouth*

Two big bison got on the boat.   *Hold up two fingers*
The rains came down,   *Fingers flutter down*
And the boat did float.   *Run fingers back and forth*
B... B... B...   *Hug yourself and rock side-to-side*
The animals played and played,   *Point fingers up on head like ears*
And Noah heard the bison say,   *Cup hand around ear*
Snort! Snort! Snort!   *Cup hands around mouth*

Number
Two

2

The Earth and the Flood

Unit 2 - Day 2

Fingerplay

Do the fingerplay *"Noah's Big Boat"*.
Focus on the sound and motion for the
letter 'B'.

<u>Key Idea</u>: 'B' = hug yourself, rock side
to side, and say *B-B*

Letter Activity

Write a big 'B' on a piece of paper.
Have students use fingerpaints,
paints and paintbrushes, or playdough
to fill in the letter.

<u>Key Idea</u>: Students will become
familiar with the shape and appearance
of the capital letter 'B'.

Bible Story

Read the Bible story from **one**
of the following resources:

✔ Scripture: Genesis 7:11-16

✔ *A Child's First Bible* p. 16-17

✔ *The New Bible in Pictures for
Little Eyes* p. 26-27

<u>Key Idea</u>: Animals got on the boat.

Bible Activity

Use the picture in the story Bible from
today's lesson. (If you read the story
directly from the Bible, you will need to
use a different source to find a picture
of the animals boarding the ark.) Have
students either count the animals by
twos, or count the total number of
animals in the picture. Then, have
students say the names of the animals
and point out any stripes, spots, or
patterns in the pictured animals.
Younger students may practice naming
the colors they see.

<u>Key Idea</u>: God brought the animals to
the ark.

Dramatic Play

Have students pretend to be animals
following God's direction to get on the
ark. You are the lead animal.
Students mimic your animal actions
and follow where you lead. Suggested
animals include the following:
galloping horses, buzzing bees,
stomping elephants, hopping
kangaroos, swinging chimpanzees,
flying hummingbirds, and tall giraffes.

<u>Key Idea</u>: God created all the animals,
and they must obey him.

Corresponding Music

The Singing Bible, Disc 1 - Track 7
Song Title: *"Noah Build a Boat"*

Hide and Seek 'B'

Two big bears got on the boat.

The rains came down,

And the boat did float.

B... B... B...

B _____ b

B _____ b

The Earth and the Flood

Fingerplay

Do the fingerplay *"Noah's Big Boat"*. Focus on the sound and motion for the letter 'B'.

<u>Key Idea</u>: 'B' = hug yourself, rock side to side, and say *B-B*

Bible Story

Read the Bible story from **one** of the following resources:

✔ Scripture: Genesis 7:17-23

✔ *A Child's First Bible* p. 18-19

✔ *The New Bible in Pictures for Little Eyes* p. 28-29

<u>Key Idea</u>: It rained for forty days.

Active Exploration

Fill a tub or sink with water. Gather items for students to test which ones float and which ones sink. Show results in a "T chart" by putting a piece of masking tape up and down and making heading cards that say "sink" and "float". As each item is tested, put it under its matching heading. Possible test items include a coin, cotton ball, paper clip, paper fastener, rock, popsicle stick, small block, plastic lid, spoon, and button.

<u>Key Idea</u>: God told Noah how to build the ark so it would float.

Letter Activity

Copy the *Hide and Seek 'B'* page. Have students circle, color, highlight, or point to the 'B's' on the page. Younger students may need help in order to find any 'B's' at all. It is not necessary to find all the 'B's'. On the bottom of the page, have students connect 'B' to 'b' by tracing the dotted line from left to right.

<u>Key Idea</u>: Students should eventually recognize the capital and small letter 'B' within words.

Bible Activity

Copy *Count on Me* (in Appendix). Direct students to draw raindrops by making a blue oval in each box. Younger students make 1 raindrop in each box. Older students make 2 raindrops in each box. Point to each raindrop as you count it with the students. Write the numbers on the lines below each box as you count. Say the numbers below the boxes to count by 1's or by 2's (counting either '1', '2', '3' ... or '2', '4', '6' ...).

<u>Key Idea</u>: God took care of Noah and his family during the flood.

Corresponding Music

The Singing Bible, Disc 1 - Track 7
Song Title: *"Noah Build a Boat"*

The Earth and the Flood

Fingerplay

Do the fingerplay *"Noah's Big Boat"*. Focus on the sound and motion for the letter 'B'.

Key Idea: 'B' = hug yourself, rock side to side, and say *B-B*

Letter Activity

Use masking tape to make a large 'B' on the floor. Have students place blocks on the tape to trace the letter. Each time a block is placed on the tape students make the letter **sound**.

Key Idea: Each letter has a name and a sound, just like animals do. For example, a dog may be named Rover, but it makes the sound, *Ruff.*

Bible Story

Read the Bible story from **one** of the following resources:

✔ Scripture: Genesis 9:8-13

✔ *A Child's First Bible* p. 20-21

✔ *The New Bible in Pictures for Little Eyes* p. 30-31

Key Idea: The flood was over.

Bible Activity

Act out the Bible story. Have students pretend to be Noah coming out of the ark. Give the students the following directions: *Shade your eyes from the bright sun. Kneel down and feel the grass. Sniff the flowers. Swipe your hand across the sky and say, "The rainbow is God's promise". Kneel down, fold your hands, and say, "Thank you God". Hug each other.* Students may also use small toys as props to act out animals and people coming out of the ark.

Key Idea: God saved Noah and his family.

Art Activity

Provide a **variety of colored construction paper** for students to tear into small pieces. Have students **glue** the pieces on **black construction paper** to create a rainbow colored picture. The black paper may be cut into the shape of a rainbow if you choose.

Key Idea: God made a rainbow as a sign of his promise that He would never again send a flood to destroy the whole earth.

Corresponding Music

The Singing Bible, Disc 1 - Track 7
Song Title: *"Noah Build a Boat"*

The Earth and the Flood

Unit 2 - Day 5

Fingerplay

Do the fingerplay *"Noah's Big Boat"*. Focus on the sound and motion for the letter 'B'.

<u>Key Idea</u>: 'B' = hug yourself, rock side to side, and say *B-B*

Letter Activity

Use the 'B' flashcard from the Appendix. Have students trace the capital and small letter 'B's' on the flashcard with their fingers. Using the flashcard as a model, choose either sidewalk chalk or 2 crayons taped together and paper to write more 'B's'.

<u>Key Idea</u>: Practice the motions needed to make the letter 'B'.

Bible Story

Read the Bible story from **one** of the following resources:

✔ Scripture: Genesis 11:4-9

✔ *A Child's First Bible* p. 22-23

✔ *The New Bible in Pictures for Little Eyes* p. 32-33

<u>Key Idea</u>: The tower of Babel

Bible Activity

Have students jump up and down next to their stuffed animals and shout, *Yeah! I won! I'm the best. I did it all by myself.* Then, have students shake hands with their stuffed animals and pat the stuffed animal while saying, *Thanks for playing with me. God helped each of us do our best.* Ask students, *Which of these two ways does God want us to act?*

<u>Key Idea</u>: We should not try to make ourselves as great as God. He is the Creator of all of us.

Math Activity

<u>Youngers</u>: Partners use building blocks to build a tower. The partners take turns counting and adding blocks one at a time to the tower until it tumbles. <u>Olders</u>: Begin a pattern that can be continued as the students build the block tower. Start with basic patterns such as alternating colors, or two of one color and then two of a different color. Progress to harder patterns.

<u>Key Idea</u>: God stopped the building of the tower of Babel because it was built to glorify man instead of God.

Corresponding Music

None for this lesson

God Blesses Abraham

Unit 3 - Day 1

Fingerplay

Do the fingerplay *"Clippity Clippity"*. Focus on the sound and motion for the letter 'C'.

Key Idea: 'C' = tap thighs with palms of hands and say *C-C*

Bible Story

Read the Bible story from **one** of the following resources:

✔ Scripture: Genesis 12:1-5

✔ *A Child's First Bible* p. 24-25

✔ *The New Bible in Pictures for Little Eyes* p. 34-35

Key Idea: Abraham left his home.

Math Activity

Youngers: Write each student's name in capital letters. Guide students to spell their names in a whisper, a shout, a low voice, a high voice, and with a clap for each letter. Cut apart and sequence the letters.
Olders: Write each student's phone number. Guide students to clap out each number. Lead students in singing their phone numbers to the tune of *"Twinkle, Twinkle, Little Star"*. Cut apart and sequence the numbers.

Key Idea: To call home, you should know your name and phone number.

Letter Activity

Copy the 'C' flashcard found in the Appendix. Show the letter side of the flashcard to the students. Read the *Hint* aloud. Demonstrate the motion and sound for 'C'. Have the students repeat it. Review the flashcards from previous weeks.

Key Idea: Students should eventually do the motion and say the sound for each flashcard without needing a *Hint* or a demonstration from you.

Bible Activity

Copy the *Number Three* page. Have students find pieces of luggage in a magazine or catalog to cut out. Use a marker to circle, box, or outline each piece of luggage so that students have a line to follow as they cut. Have students glue the luggage on the *Number Three* page. Save this page. A page will be added each week to make a '1-10' counting book.

Key Idea: Abraham packed and left the city of Ur with his family as God told him to do.

Corresponding Music

The Singing Bible, Disc 1 - Track 8
Song Title: *"God Began a Nation"*

Fingerplay: Clippity Clippity

Days 1-5

Clippity, Clippity,	*Tap palms on thighs in rhythm*
C-C-Clack!	*Tap palms on thighs in rhythm*
God tells Abraham	*Rub chin where beard would be*
You must pack!	*Pretend to put things in suitcase*

Clippity, Clippity,	*Tap palms on thighs in rhythm*
C-C-Clop!	*Tap palms on thighs in rhythm*
God tells Abraham	*Rub chin where beard would be*
Where to stop!	*Hold hand up with palm facing out*

Clippity, Clippity,	*Tap palms on thighs in rhythm*
C-C-Clap!	*Tap palms on thighs in rhythm*
God sends Abraham's	*Rub chin where beard would be*
Son at last!	*Hold baby and rock arms*

Clippity, Clippity,	*Tap palms on thighs in rhythm*
C-C-Clomp!	*Tap palms on thighs in rhythm*
God sends Abraham's	*Rub chin where beard would be*
Blessings down!	*Wiggle fingers from above*

Number
Three

3

God Blesses Abraham

Unit 3 - Day 2

Fingerplay

Do the fingerplay *"Clippity Clippity"*. Focus on the sound and motion for the letter 'C'.

Key Idea: 'C' = tap thighs with palms of hands and say *C-C*

Letter Activity

Write a big 'C' on a piece of paper. Have students glue cotton balls or pieces of yarn to the letter. Younger students will need you to apply drops of glue on the letter for them first.

Key Idea: Students will become familiar with the shape and appearance of the capital letter 'C'.

Bible Story

Read the Bible story from **one** of the following resources:

✔ Scripture: Genesis 13:5-11, 14-15

✔ *A Child's First Bible* p. 26-27

✔ *The New Bible in Pictures for Little Eyes* p. 36-37

Key Idea: God blessed Abraham.

Bible Activity

Act out the Bible story. Set out stuffed animals or other props to be sheep. Have students say, *Baaa! Baaa!* You pretend to be Abraham. Say, *There's not enough grass. Lot, you choose where you want to live.* Instruct students to take half of the sheep and move them away. Have students kneel down as you say, *Lot took the best land, but I trust you, God, to take care of me.*

Key Idea: Abraham trusted God and let Lot choose the best land. God blessed Abraham because he wasn't selfish.

Devotional Activity

Read and discuss the devotion from **one** of the following resources:

✔ *Big Thoughts for Little People*
Read the two pages for letter 'C'.

✔ *Teach Them to Your Children*
Read the two pages for letter 'C'.

✔ *My ABC Bible Verses*
Read the two pages for letter 'C'.

Key Idea: Share a devotional focusing on character traits or memory work based on the letter 'C'.

Corresponding Music

The Singing Bible, Disc 1 - Track 8
Song Title: *"God Began a Nation"*

God Blesses Abraham

Fingerplay

Do the fingerplay *"Clippity Clippity"*. Focus on the sound and motion for the letter 'C'.

<u>Key Idea</u>: 'C' = tap thighs with palms of hands and say *C-C*

Letter Activity

Use masking tape to make a large 'C' on the floor. Have students drive a toy car or other toy vehicle on the tape to trace the letter. Have students say the letter **sound** as they drive.

<u>Key Idea</u>: Each letter has a name and a sound, just like animals do. For example, a horse may be named Silver, but it makes the sound, *Neigh.*

Bible Story

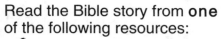

Read the Bible story from **one** of the following resources:

✔ Scripture: Genesis 15:3-6

✔ *A Child's First Bible* p. 28-29 (plus the Scripture listed above)

✔ *The New Bible in Pictures for Little Eyes* p. 38-39

<u>Key Idea</u>: God made a promise to Abraham.

Bible Activity

Use a blanket or other prop as a tent. Have students wear bathrobes or drape towels over their shoulders to show Abraham's robe. Turn the lights off and have students crawl into the tent. Read Genesis 15:3-6 and act out Abraham talking to God. Tell students to come out of the tent and point up to count the stars. Have students stop counting and thank God for his promise.

<u>Key Idea</u>: God made a covenant with Abraham, and Abraham believed and trusted God.

Art Activity

Have students draw and **color** bright stripes on an **index card**. Fold the card in half to be a tent. Have students dip a wadded up **paper towel** in **white tempera paint**. Tell students to press the paper towel on **black paper** to create white stars in a night sky. Help students tape the tent to the black paper with **clear tape.**

<u>Key Idea</u>: God promised Abraham a son and more children than the stars in the sky.

Corresponding Music

The Singing Bible, Disc 1 - Track 8
Song Title: *"God Began a Nation"*

God Blesses Abraham

Unit 3 - Day 4

Fingerplay

Do the fingerplay *"Clippity Clippity"*. Focus on the sound and motion for the letter 'C'.

Key Idea: 'C' = tap thighs with palms of hands and say *C-C*

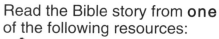

Bible Story

Read the Bible story from **one** of the following resources:

✔ Scripture: Genesis 18:1-10

✔ *A Child's First Bible* p. 28-29 (plus the Scripture listed above)

✔ *The New Bible in Pictures for Little Eyes* p. 40-41

Key Idea: Three men from heaven

Dramatic Play

Lay a blanket or towel on the floor. Set out 3 stuffed animals to be the 3 guests that visited Abraham. Have students pretend to be Abraham as they count and pass out a plate to each guest. Tell students to count and pass out spoons, napkins, cups, and snacks. Pour juice for the guests. For older children, emphasize proper place settings and table manners.

Key Idea: Even though Abraham was very old, he trusted God to give him a son.

Letter Activity

Copy the *Hide and Seek 'C'* page. Have students circle, color, highlight, or point to the 'C's' on the page. Younger students may need help finding any 'C's' at all. It is not necessary to find all the 'C's'. On the bottom of the page, have students connect 'C' to 'c' by tracing the dotted line from left to right.

Key Idea: Students should eventually recognize the capital and small letter 'C' within words.

Bible Activity

Copy *Count on Me* (in Appendix). Direct students to draw tents by making a brown upside-down 'V' shape in the boxes. Younger students make 1 tent in each box. Older students make 2 tents in each box. Point to each tent as you count it with the students. Write the numbers on the lines below each box as you count. Say the numbers below the boxes to count by 1's or by 2's (counting either '1', '2', '3' ... or '2', '4', '6' ...).

Key Idea: Three men from heaven visited Abraham in the desert.

Corresponding Music

The Singing Bible, Disc 1 - Track 8
Song Title: *"God Began a Nation"*

Hide and Seek 'C'

Clippity, Clippity,

C-C-Clack!

God tells Abraham

You must pack!

C   ------------------------------------   C

C   ------------------------------------   C

God Blesses Abraham

Unit 3 - Day 5

Fingerplay

Do the fingerplay *"Clippity Clippity"*. Focus on the sound and motion for the letter 'C'.

Key Idea: 'C' = tap thighs with palms of hands and say *C-C*

Bible Story

Read the Bible story from **one** of the following resources:

✔ Scripture: Genesis 22:1-3, 9-13
✔ *The New Bible in Pictures for Little Eyes* p. 42-43

Key Idea: God tested Abraham.

Active Exploration

Look at baby pictures of your students. Discuss how they have changed. Point out differences such as the changing size of their hands and feet, crawling vs. walking, bottle feeding vs. feeding themselves, and baby talk vs. real words. Have students tell you any changes they notice. Invite students to share stories about silly things they did when they were younger or about the first time they did something.

Key Idea: Abraham's son, Isaac, grew up and changed too.

Letter Activity

Use the 'C' flashcard from the Appendix. Have students trace the capital and small letter 'C' on the flashcard with their fingers. Using the flashcard as a model, give students either a small amount of cooking oil or liquid soap on an aluminum pan or plate to use to write more 'C's'.

Key Idea: Practice the motions needed to make the letter 'C'.

Bible Activity

Set out some of the students' favorite toys along with a Bible. Have students hug the toys and say, *I love you more than anything.* Then, have students hug the Bible and say, *I love you, Lord, more than anything.* Ask students, *Which of these two ways does God want us to act? How can we show God that we love him?*

Key Idea: Abraham proved that he loved God even more than he loved his son, Isaac.

Corresponding Music

The Singing Bible, Disc 1 - Track 8
Song Title: *"God Began a Nation"*

erenstaln- pg 44-47
kumon
Little Red Hen

Isaac and His Sons

Fingerplay

Do the fingerplay *"One Dusty Camel"*. Focus on the sound and motion for the letter 'D'.

Key Idea: 'D' = pretend to hold the reins of a camel, move up and down, and say *D-D*

Letter Activity

Copy the 'D' flashcard found in the Appendix. Show the letter side of the flashcard to the students. Read the *Hint* aloud. Demonstrate the motion and sound for 'D'. Have the students repeat it. Review the flashcards from previous weeks.

Key Idea: Students should eventually do the motion and say the sound for each flashcard without needing a *Hint* or a demonstration from you.

Bible Story

Read the Bible story from **one** of the following resources:

✔ Scripture: Genesis 24:1-7, 61-67

✔ *A Child's First Bible* p. 30

✔ *The New Bible in Pictures for Little Eyes* p. 44-47

Key Idea: Isaac met Rebekah.

Bible Activity

Copy the *Number Four* page. Have students find four women in a magazine or catalog to cut out. Use a marker to circle, box, or outline each woman so that students have a line to follow as they cut. Have students glue the women on the *Number Four* page. Save this page. A page will be added each week to make a '1-10' counting book.

Key Idea: Rebekah said she would marry Isaac.

Active Exploration

Give students these directions: *Meet your stuffed animal for the first time, shake hands, and tell it your name. Move the animal's head and arms as you tell it your answers to the following questions: "How old are you?" "What foods do you like to eat?" "What do you like to play?"* Have students take the animal on a tour of the surrounding area.

Key Idea: Isaac and Rebekah needed to get to know each other, since they had never met.

Corresponding Music

None for this lesson

Fingerplay: One Dusty Camel

Days 1-5

One dusty camel	*Hold up 1 finger*
In the desert heat,	*Fan yourself with one hand*
One dusty camel	*Hold up 1 finger*
Took Rebekah to meet,	*Shake hands with someone*
Isaac near the field	*Sweep hand in front of you*
In the desert heat.	*Fan yourself with one hand*
D-D-D-D	*Hold reins of camel and move up-down-up-down*

One dusty camel	*Hold up 1 finger*
In the desert heat,	*Fan yourself with one hand*
One dusty camel	*Hold up 1 finger*
Took Jacob to meet,	*Shake hands with someone*
Rachel near the well	*Sweep hand in front of you*
In the desert heat.	*Fan yourself with one hand*
D-D-D-D	*Hold reins of camel and move up-down-up-down*

One dusty camel	*Hold up 1 finger*
In the desert heat,	*Fan yourself with one hand*
One dusty camel	*Hold up 1 finger*
Took Esau to meet,	*Shake hands with someone*
Jacob near the river	*Sweep hand in front of you*
In the desert heat.	*Fan yourself with one hand*
D-D-D-D	*Hold reins of camel and move up-down-up-down*

Number
Four

4

Isaac and His Sons

Unit 4 - Day 2

Fingerplay

Do the fingerplay *"One Dusty Camel"*. Focus on the sound and motion for the letter 'D'.

<u>Key Idea</u>: 'D' = pretend to hold the reins of a camel, move up and down, and say *D-D*

Letter Activity

Use masking tape to make a large 'D' on the floor. Have students tiptoe on the tape to trace the letter. Then, have students jump off the end of the letter saying the letter **sound** as they jump.

<u>Key Idea</u>: Each letter has a name and a sound, just like animals do. For example, a cow may be named Bessie, but it makes the sound, *Moo.*

Bible Story

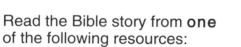

Read the Bible story from **one** of the following resources:

 Scripture: Genesis 27:15-24

 *A Child's First Bible* p. 32

✔ *The New Bible in Pictures for Little Eyes* p. 48-49

<u>Key Idea</u>: Jacob lied to his father.

Bible Activity

Act out the Bible story. The students pretend to be Jacob. You pretend to be Isaac. Jacob kneels in front of you. Feel Jacob's arms, smell his clothes, eat the meat Jacob has prepared, then bless him. Redo the scene, but this time have Jacob say, *I am not Esau. I was trying to get the blessing.* Hug Jacob and say, *I'm glad you told the truth.* Ask students, *Which of these two ways does God want us to act?*

<u>Key Idea</u>: It is better to be truthful.

Art Activity

Use **black marker** to make a dotted outline of each student's name on **white paper**. Then, have students trace over the dotted outlines to write their names. Have students draw and **color** designs over their names to try to camouflage or hide them.

<u>Key Idea</u>: Jacob tried to hide who he was by pretending to be Esau. It is better to be yourself. God has blessings planned for each of us.

Corresponding Music

The Singing Bible, Disc 1 - Track 9
Song Title: *"The Blessing That Will Be"*

Hide and Seek 'D'

One dusty camel

Took Rebekah to meet,

Isaac near the field

In the desert heat.

D... D... D... D...

D _____ d

D _____ d

Berenstain pg. 50-51
Kumon
Little Red Hen
Yellow Cake- Bake

Fingerplay

Do the fingerplay *"One Dusty Camel"*. Focus on the sound and motion for the letter 'D'.

Key Idea: 'D' = pretend to hold the reins of a camel, move up and down, and say *D-D*

Letter Activity

Copy the *Hide and Seek 'D'* page. Have students circle, color, highlight, or point to the 'D's' on the page. Younger students may need help finding any 'D's' at all. It is not necessary to find all the 'D's'. On the bottom of the page, have students connect 'D' to 'd' by tracing the dotted line from left to right.

Key Idea: Students should eventually recognize the capital and small letter 'D' within words.

Bible Story

Read the Bible story from **one** of the following resources:

✔ Scripture: Genesis 28:10-15, 29:16-20

✔ *A Child's First Bible* p. 31 (plus the Scripture listed above)

✔ *The New Bible in Pictures for Little Eyes* p. 50-53

Key Idea: Jacob left home.

Bible Activity

Copy *Count on Me* (in Appendix). Direct students to draw ladders by making a brown 'H' in the boxes. Younger students make 1 ladder in each box. Older students make 2 ladders in each box. Point to each ladder as you count it with the students. Write the numbers on the lines below each box as you count. Say the numbers below the boxes to count by 1's or by 2's (counting either '1', '2', '3' ... or '2', '4', '6' ...).

Key Idea: Jacob dreamt of a ladder.

Math Activity

Use a strip of masking tape on the floor as a starting line. Set a doll or stuffed animal quite a distance in front of the line to be Rachel. Have students stand behind the line and jump toward Rachel. Use a small piece of tape to mark each jump. Compare the jumps using words such as *shorter, farther,* and *closest.*

Key Idea: Jacob traveled a long distance before he met Rachel.

Corresponding Music

The Singing Bible, Disc 1 - Track 9
Song Title: *"The Blessing That Will Be"*

Berenstain- pg52-53
HW-21-22
Quilt Square

Isaac and His Sons

Fingerplay

Do the fingerplay *"One Dusty Camel"*. Focus on the sound and motion for the letter 'D'.

Key Idea: 'D' = pretend to hold the reins of a camel, move up and down, and say *D-D*

Letter Activity

Write a big 'D' on a piece of paper. Have students glue dried macaroni or raisins to the letter. Younger students will need you to apply drops of glue on the letter for them first.

Key Idea: Students will become familiar with the shape and appearance of the capital letter 'D'.

Bible Story

Read the Bible story from **one** of the following resources:

✔ Scripture: Genesis 32:22-31

✔ *The New Bible in Pictures for Little Eyes* p. 54-55

Key Idea: Jacob wrestled an angel.

Bible Activity

Act out the Bible story. Tell students to choose two toys or stuffed animals to wrestle each other. Name one Jacob and the other one the angel. Have students make the toys wrestle back and forth until the angel touches Jacob's leg, so Jacob can't use that leg anymore. Have the angel say, *Stop, Jacob!* Have Jacob say, *I won't stop until you bless me.* Make the angel bless Jacob.

Key Idea: Jacob wrestled with the angel all night to win God's blessing. Do you ask God to bless you?

Dramatic Play

Inflate a balloon to be "wrestled back and forth" between partners pretending to be Jacob and the angel. The partners take turns batting the balloon to keep it from touching the floor. Count each time the balloon is hit. Have partners do the same activity sitting down. Point out how hard it is to "wrestle the balloon" without using your legs.

Key Idea: Jacob wanted God's blessing so much he kept wrestling no matter how hard it got.

Corresponding Music

The Singing Bible, Disc 1 - Track 9
Song Title: *"The Blessing That Will Be"*

Isaac and His Sons

Unit 4 - Day 5

Fingerplay

Do the fingerplay *"One Dusty Camel"*. Focus on the sound and motion for the letter 'D'.

<u>Key Idea</u>: 'D' = pretend to hold the reins of a camel, move up and down, and say *D-D*

Letter Activity

Use the 'D' flashcard from the Appendix. Have students trace the capital and small letter 'D' on the flashcard with their fingers. Using the flashcard as a model, choose either pudding, chocolate syrup, baby food, or fingerpaint on a plate, pan, or piece of paper for students to write more 'D's'.

<u>Key Idea</u>: Practice the motions needed to make the letter 'D'.

Bible Story

Read the Bible story from **one** of the following resources:

✔ Scripture: Genesis 33:1-7

✔ *A Child's First Bible* p. 33

✔ *The New Bible in Pictures for Little Eyes* p. 56-57

<u>Key Idea</u>: Esau forgave Jacob.

Bible Activity

Act out the Bible story. Have students be Jacob. Use a stuffed animal to be Esau. Give students the following directions: *Pretend to get on a camel and ride slowly, moving up and down. Point and say, "There's Esau. I wonder if he is still mad?" Get off the camel. Bow down seven times in front of Esau. Say, "I am sorry. Can you forgive me?" Have Esau nod his head up and down and hug you.*

<u>Key Idea</u>: Esau forgave Jacob. God blessed both brothers.

Devotional Activity

Read and discuss the devotion from **one** of the following resources:

✔ *Big Thoughts for Little People*
Read the two pages for letter 'D'.

✔ *Teach Them to Your Children*
Read the two pages for letter 'D'.

✔ *My ABC Bible Verses*
Read the two pages for letter 'D'.

<u>Key Idea</u>: Share a devotional focusing on character traits or memory work based on the letter 'D'.

Corresponding Music

The Singing Bible, Disc 1 - Track 9
Song Title: *"The Blessing That Will Be"*

Young Joseph

Fingerplay

Do the fingerplay *"What Do You Know?"* Focus on reviewing the sounds and motions for the letters.

Key Idea: Practice the sounds and motions for the letters 'A-D'.

Bible Story

Read the Bible story from **one** of the following resources:

✔ Scripture: Genesis 37:3-4

✔ *A Child's First Bible* p. 34

✔ *The New Bible in Pictures for Little Eyes* p. 58-59

Key Idea: Joseph's father gave him a special coat.

Art Activity

Have students use **Q-Tips** to paint colorful stripes on a **coffee filter, napkin,** or **paper towel**. Tell students to dip the Q-Tip in **tempera paint** first, and then dip it in **water** before making stripes on the filter, napkin, or paper towel. This creates a colorful watery effect. Students should use a different Q-Tip for each color of **paint**. Water colored with food coloring may be used in place of paint.

Key Idea: Jacob loved Joseph and gave him a colorful coat as a gift.

Letter Activity

This is a review week. Review all the flashcards from the previous weeks. Show the letter side of each flashcard to the students. Have them respond with the motion and sound. If needed, read the *Hint* or demonstrate the motion and sound.

Key Idea: Students should eventually do the motion and say the sound for each flashcard without needing a *Hint* or a demonstration from you.

Bible Activity

Give students the following directions: *Pretend to be Joseph opening a present. Act surprised and say, "A new coat?" Stand up and pretend to put the coat on. Twirl around in excitement. Say, "Thank you Dad. I love all the colors".* Have students tell about a special present they received. Ask students, *Have you ever been jealous of a present someone else received? What does God say we should do?*

Key Idea: Joseph's brothers were jealous of Joseph's special coat.

Corresponding Music

The Singing Bible, Disc 1 - Track 10
Song Title: *"Joseph's Dream"*

Fingerplay: What Do You Know?

Days 1-5

We've learned about *A-A-Adam*	*Hands on cheeks in surprise*
And *B-B-Boat,*	*Hug yourself and rock side-to-side*
C-C-Clippity clop	*Tap palms on thighs in rhythm*
And *D-D-Dusty* camel.	*Hold reins; move up and down*
Now, as Joseph	*Hold hands together as if cuffed*
Is taken away,	*Walk fingers up arm*
God trains Joseph	*Point up*
To lead someday.	*Motion with hand to follow you*
Just like the others	*Open palms together like Bible*
God has plans for you too.	*Point up, then point to yourself*
Never forget	*Shake head, "No"*
What God can do!	*Spread arms wide*

Young Joseph

Fingerplay

Do the fingerplay *"What Do You Know?"* Focus on reviewing the sounds and motions for the letters.

Key Idea: Practice the sounds and motions for the letters 'A-D'.

Letter Activity

Choose one or more of the letters 'A-D' to review. Use masking tape to make the large review letter on the floor. Have students sit on a pillow and scoot on the tape to trace the letter. Have students say the letter **sound** as they scoot.

Key Idea: Each letter has a name and a sound, just like animals do. For example, a pig may be named Pinky, but it makes the sound, *Oink.*

Bible Story

Read the Bible story from **one** of the following resources:

✔ Scripture: Genesis 37:13, 18-24

✔ *The New Bible in Pictures for Little Eyes* p. 60-61

Key Idea: Joseph went to find his brothers.

Bible Activity

Copy *Count on Me* (in Appendix). Direct students to draw stripes by making different colored lines in the boxes. Younger students make 1 stripe in each box. Older students make 2 stripes in each box. Point to each stripe as you count it with the students. Write the numbers on the lines below each box as you count. Say the numbers below the boxes to count by 1's or 2's (counting either '1', '2', '3'... or '2', '4', '6' ...).

Key Idea: Joseph's brothers were jealous of his special striped coat.

Devotional Activity

Read and discuss the devotion from **one** of the following resources:

✔ *Big Thoughts for Little People*
Review verses for 'A', 'B', 'C', 'D'

✔ *Teach Them to Your Children*
Review verses for 'A', 'B', 'C', 'D'

✔ *My ABC Bible Verses*
Review verses for 'A', 'B', 'C', 'D'

Key Idea: Share a devotional focusing on character traits or memory work based on the letters 'A', 'B', 'C', 'D'.

Corresponding Music

The Singing Bible, Disc 1 - Track 10
Song Title: *"Joseph's Dream"*

Young Joseph

Fingerplay

Do the fingerplay *"What Do You Know?"* Focus on reviewing the sounds and motions for the letters.

Key Idea: Practice the sounds and motions for the letters 'A-D'.

Bible Story

Read the Bible story from **one** of the following resources:

✔ Scripture: Genesis 37:28-34

✔ *A Child's First Bible* p. 35 (plus the Scripture listed above)

✔ *The New Bible in Pictures for Little Eyes* p. 62-63

Key Idea: Joseph was sold.

Math Activity

Youngers: Lay coins on a flat surface and tape white paper on top. Have students rub the flat side of a crayon over the coins. Name the coins.
Olders: Have students sort pennies, nickels, dimes, and quarters into different compartments of a muffin tin. Help students count the coins in each tin. Say the coin names with the students.

Key Idea: Joseph's brothers were jealous, so they sold him for money.

Letter Activity

Copy the *Hide-n-Seek Review* page. Choose a letter from 'A-D' for students to review. Have students circle, color, highlight, or point to the chosen letter. Younger students may need help in order to find any of the chosen letters. On the bottom of the page, have students draw a line to connect each capital letter to its matching lowercase letter.

Key Idea: Students should eventually recognize the capital and small letters 'A-D' within words.

Bible Activity

Copy the *Number Five* page. Have students find five purses or wallets in a magazine or catalog to cut out. Use a marker to circle, box, or outline each purse or wallet so that students have a line to follow as they cut. Have students glue the purses or wallets on the *Number Five* page. Save this page. A page will be added each week to make a '1-10' counting book.

Key Idea: Joseph was sold to be a slave, but God was with him.

Corresponding Music

The Singing Bible, Disc 1 - Track 10 Song Title: *"Joseph's Dream"*

Hide and Seek Review

We've learned about A-A-Adam,

And B-B-Boat,

C-C-Clippity clop,

And D-D-Dusty Camel.

A

B

C

D

b

a

d

c

Number
Five

5

Young Joseph

Fingerplay

Do the fingerplay *"What Do You Know?"* Focus on reviewing the sounds and motions for the letters.

<u>Key Idea</u>:   Practice the sounds and motions for the letters 'A-D'.

Bible Story

Read the Bible story from **one** of the following resources:

✔ Scripture: Genesis 39:1-5

✔ *The New Bible in Pictures for Little Eyes* p. 64-65

<u>Key Idea</u>:   Joseph worked in Egypt.

Active Exploration

Ask students, *How well can you follow directions?* Let students choose one of their favorite toys. Pretend the toys are talking to the students as they give the following directions: *Lift me above your head. Slide me around your waist. Put me behind your back. Set me beside you on the floor. Jump me over your foot. Swing me under your arm. Set me near another person. Walk me 5 steps toward the door. Hold me away from your body.*

<u>Key Idea</u>:   Joseph was put in charge of telling others what to do.

Letter Activity

Choose one letter from 'A-D' to review. Write that letter on a big piece of paper. Use water to thin glue and have students "paint" the glue on the letter. Then, sprinkle either salt, coffee grounds, glitter, or any kind of spice on the glue. Younger students will need you to help them with the sprinkling part.

<u>Key Idea</u>:   Students will become familiar with the shape and appearance of the capital letters.

Bible Activity

Have the following discussion with the students: *When are some times that you are alone? How would you feel if you had to leave your family and live somewhere else? God watches over us like a father. He is always with us, so we are never all alone. The next time you feel alone, pray and thank God for being with you. Then, you won't feel so alone. Let's pray about it right now.*

<u>Key Idea</u>:   Joseph lived in Egypt far away from his family, but God was with him.

Corresponding Music

The Singing Bible, Disc 1 - Track 10
Song Title: *"Joseph's Dream"*

Young Joseph

Unit 5 - Day 5

Fingerplay

Do the fingerplay *"What Do You Know?"* Focus on reviewing the sounds and motions for the letters.

Key Idea: Practice the sounds and motions for the letters 'A-D'.

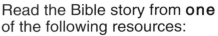

Bible Story

Read the Bible story from **one** of the following resources:

 Scripture: Genesis 39:20-22

 The New Bible in Pictures for Little Eyes p. 66-67

Key Idea: God took care of Joseph in prison.

Dramatic Play

Have students nod their toys' heads, *Yes* or *No,* to show the students' responses to each of the following statements: *Your hair is red. You like candy. You like to color. You have brothers or sisters. You are 7 years old. You have a pet. God loves you.* Older students can make up statements and give you a chance to respond, instead.

Key Idea: Joseph was in prison because someone said he did something bad, but that was not true.

Letter Activity

Choose one or more of the flashcards from the previous weeks to review. Have students trace the capital and small letters on the flashcards with their fingers. Using the flashcards as models, choose either markers and markerboards or pieces of carpet and fingers to practice writing more letters.

Key Idea: Practice the motions needed to make the letters.

Bible Activity

Have students answer, *Yes, Mom,* or, *Yes, teacher,* as they pantomime each of the following things: *Put away your toys. Sit and wait quietly. Close the door softly. Make your bed. Get dressed.* Ask students, *Do you work hard even when you don't like what you've been asked to do? Do you listen to what God tells you in the Bible, or do you do what you want instead?*

Key Idea: Joseph worked hard even when he was in prison, and God watched over him.

Corresponding Music

None for this lesson

Joseph Becomes a Leader

Fingerplay

Do the fingerplay *"Joseph's Brothers"*. Focus on the sound and motion for the letter 'E'.

Key Idea: 'E' = pretend to shake an empty jar upside down and say *E-E*

Letter Activity

Copy the 'E' flashcard found in the Appendix. Show the letter side of the flashcard to the students. Read the *Hint* aloud. Demonstrate the motion and sound for 'E'. Have the students repeat it.

Key Idea: Students should eventually do the motion and say the sound for each flashcard without needing a *Hint* or a demonstration from you.

Bible Story

Read the Bible story from **one** of the following resources:

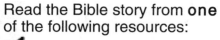
 Scripture: Genesis 41:14-16, 28-32

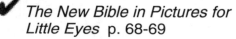 *The New Bible in Pictures for Little Eyes* p. 68-69

Key Idea: The king had a dream.

Bible Activity

Copy the *Number Six* page. Have students find six pillows or blankets in a magazine or catalog to cut out. Use a marker to circle, box, or outline each pillow or blanket so that students have a line to follow as they cut. Have students glue the pillows or blankets on the *Number Six* page. Save this page. A page will be added each week to make a '1-10' counting book.

Key Idea: The king had a dream. God told Joseph what the dream meant, so Joseph could save Egypt and his own family from starving.

Dramatic Play

Pair students up. One person in each pair sits with his back to his partner. The partner moves his fingers on the other person's back like a worm, a bunny, or an elephant. Then, the person guesses which animal it is. Continue playing by taking turns. Older students may add animals such as a spider, a fish, or a porcupine. Say, *It is hard to explain something we can't see.*

Key Idea: God helped Joseph explain the king's dream, even though Joseph didn't see the dream.

Corresponding Music

The Singing Bible, Disc 1 - Track 11
Song Title: *"Seven Fat Cows"*

Fingerplay: Joseph's Brothers

Days 1-5

One empty,	*Hold up 1 finger*
Two empty,	*Hold up 3 fingers*
E-E-E	*Shake hand to shake empty jar*
Four empty,	*Hold up 4 fingers*
Five empty,	*Hold up 5 fingers*
Six empty jars.	*Hold up 6 fingers*
E-E-E	*Shake hand to shake empty jar*
Seven empty,	*Hold up 7 fingers*
Eight empty,	*Hold up 8 fingers*
Nine empty jars.	*Hold up 9 fingers*
E-E-E	*Shake hand to shake empty jar*
No grain for eating	*Shake head, "No"*
We don't want to starve!	*Rub tummy*

One brother,	*Hold up 1 finger*
Two brothers,	*Hold up 2 fingers*
Three brothers,	*Hold up 3 fingers*
Four.	*Hold up 4 fingers*
Five brothers,	*Hold up 5 fingers*
Six brothers,	*Hold up 6 fingers*
Seven brothers more.	*Hold up 7 fingers*
Eight brothers,	*Hold up 8 fingers*
Nine brothers,	*Hold up 9 fingers*
Here is ten!	*Hold up 10 fingers*
And one more brother	*Hold up 1 finger*
Named Benjamin.	

One bowing,	*Hold up 1 finger*
Two bowing,	*Hold up 2 fingers*
Three bowing,	*Hold up 3 fingers*
Four.	*Hold up 4 fingers*
Five bowing,	*Hold up 5 fingers*
Six bowing,	*Hold up 6 fingers*
Seven bowing down.	*Hold up 7 fingers make them bow*
Eight bowing,	*Hold up 8 fingers*
Nine bowing,	*Hold up 9 fingers*
Ten, eleven too.	*Hold up 10 fingers, and 1 more*
Joseph, we can't believe	
It's you!	*Cover mouth with hands*

Fingerplay: Joseph's Brothers

Days 1-5

One empty,	*Hold up 1 finger*
Two empty,	*Hold up 2 fingers*
Three empty jars.	*Hold up 3 fingers*
E-E-E	*Shake hand to shake empty jar*
Four empty,	*Hold up 4 fingers*
Five empty,	*Hold up 5 fingers*
Six empty jars.	*Hold up 6 fingers*
E-E-E	*Shake hand to shake empty jar*
Seven empty,	*Hold up 7 fingers*
Eight empty,	*Hold up 8 fingers*
Nine empty jars.	*Hold up 9 fingers*
E-E-E	*Shake hand to shake empty jar*
No grain for eating	*Shake head, "No"*
We don't want to starve!	*Rub tummy*
One brother,	*Hold up 1 finger*
Two brothers,	*Hold up 2 fingers*
Three brothers,	*Hold up 3 fingers*
Four.	*Hold up 4 fingers*
Five brothers,	*Hold up 5 fingers*
Six brothers,	*Hold up 6 fingers*
Seven brothers more.	*Hold up 7 fingers*
Eight brothers,	*Hold up 8 fingers*
Nine brothers,	*Hold up 9 fingers*
Here are ten!	*Hold up 10 fingers*
And one more brother	*Hold up 1 finger*
Named Benjamin.	
One bowing,	*Hold up 1 finger*
Two bowing,	*Hold up 2 fingers*
Three bowing,	*Hold up 3 fingers*
Four.	*Hold up 4 fingers*
Five bowing,	*Hold up 5 fingers*
Six bowing,	*Hold up 6 fingers*
Seven bowing down.	*Hold up 7 fingers make them bow*
Eight bowing,	*Hold up 8 fingers*
Nine bowing,	*Hold up 9 fingers*
Ten, eleven too.	*Hold up 10 fingers, and 1 more*
Joseph, we can't believe	
It's you!	*Cover mouth with hands*

Number
Six

Joseph Becomes a Leader

Unit 6 - Day 2

Fingerplay

Do the fingerplay *"Joseph's Brothers"*. Focus on the sound and motion for the letter 'E'.

Key Idea: 'E' = pretend to shake an empty jar upside down and say *E-E*

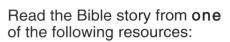

Bible Story

Read the Bible story from **one** of the following resources:

✔ Scripture: Genesis 41:38-41, 46-49

✔ *The New Bible in Pictures for Little Eyes* p. 70-71

Key Idea: Everyone obeyed Joseph.

Math Activity

Play *"Joseph, May I?"* Students line up on one side of the room with you, Joseph, on the other side. Students take turns saying, *Joseph, May I?* Answer by telling each student how many of a certain kind of step to take. Possible kinds of steps are ant steps, dinosaur steps, frog steps, snail steps, and penguin steps. When students reach you, they should bow down.

Key Idea: The king put Joseph in charge of the land of Egypt.

Letter Activity

Copy the *Hide and Seek 'E'* page. Have students circle, color, highlight, or point to the 'E's' on the page. Younger students may need help in order to find any 'E's' at all. It is not necessary to find all the 'E's'. On the bottom of the page, have students connect 'E' to 'e' by tracing the dotted line from left to right.

Key Idea: Students should eventually recognize the capital and small letter 'E' within words.

Bible Activity

Copy *Count on Me* (in Appendix). Direct students to draw rings by making a circle with a colored dot on top in each box. Younger students make 1 ring in each box. Older students make 2 rings in each box. Point to each ring as you count it. Write the numbers on the lines below each box as you count. Say the numbers below the boxes to count by 1's or by 2's (counting either '1', '2', '3'... or '2', '4', '6' ...).

Key Idea: The king gave Joseph a ring to show Joseph was important.

Corresponding Music

The Singing Bible, Disc 1 - Track 11
Song Title: *"Seven Fat Cows"*

Hide and Seek 'E'

One empty,

Two empty,

Three empty jars.

E... E... E...

E ------------------------------------ e

E ------------------------------------ e

Joseph Becomes a Leader

Fingerplay

Do the fingerplay *"Joseph's Brothers"*. Focus on the sound and motion for the letter 'E'.

Key Idea: 'E' = pretend to shake an empty jar upside down and say *E-E*

Bible Story

Read the Bible story from **one** of the following resources:

 Scripture: Genesis 42:3-8

 The New Bible in Pictures for Little Eyes p. 72-73

Key Idea: Joseph helped his brothers.

Art Activity

On **brown construction paper** have students draw and **color** a person, no larger than a sticky note, with an Egyptian headdress. Place a **sticky note** over the person. **Thin glue with water** for students to spread on the brown paper. Sprinkle **salt** or **sugar** over the glue to make sparkly desert sand. Older students may add pyramids made from index cards folded like tents. Lift the sticky note to see Joseph.

Key Idea: Joseph's brothers didn't recognize him at first.

Letter Activity

Use masking tape to make a large 'E' on the floor. Have students walk a stuffed animal on the tape to trace the letter. Then, have students walk the letter themselves, saying the letter **sound** as they walk.

Key Idea: Each letter has a name and a sound, just like animals do. For example, a bunny may be named Cottontail, but it makes the sound, *Squeak.*

Bible Activity

Act out the Bible story. Pretend you are Joseph. Line up ten stuffed toys to be Joseph's ten brothers traveling to Egypt. Help students count the ten brothers. Have students help each brother get off his imaginary camel and bow down in front of you. Ask the brothers, *Why have you come?* The brothers say, *We have come for food.*

Key Idea: God helped Joseph forgive his brothers, and Joseph gave them the food they needed.

Corresponding Music

The Singing Bible, Disc 1 - Track 11
Song Title: *"Seven Fat Cows"*

Joseph Becomes a Leader

Fingerplay

Do the fingerplay *"Joseph's Brothers"*. Focus on the sound and motion for the letter 'E'.

Key Idea: 'E' = pretend to shake an empty jar upside down and say *E-E*

Bible Story

Read the Bible story from **one** of the following resources:

✔ Scripture: Genesis 45:4-10

✔ *The New Bible in Pictures for Little Eyes* p. 74-75

Key Idea: Joseph forgave his brothers.

Devotional Activity

Read and discuss the devotion from **one** of the following resources:

✔ *Big Thoughts for Little People*
Read the two pages for letter 'E'.

✔ *Teach Them to Your Children*
Read the two pages for letter 'E'.

✔ *My ABC Bible Verses*
Read the two pages for letter 'E'.

Key Idea: Share a devotional focusing on character traits or memory work based on the letter 'E'.

Letter Activity

Write a big 'E' on a piece of paper. Have students glue dry 'O'-shaped cereal or dried beans to the letter. Younger students will need you to apply drops of glue on the letter for them first.

Key Idea: Students will become familiar with the shape and appearance of the capital letter 'E'.

Bible Activity

Ask students, *What would we notice about you, if we looked more closely?* Say, *For example, you might have eyes that are the same color as your mother's or father's eyes. You might have a scar from a fall. You might wear glasses or be missing a tooth. Maybe you have freckles or a special mole.* Have students share things that they notice about themselves.

Key Idea: Joseph's brothers didn't recognize him until they looked more closely.

Corresponding Music

The Singing Bible, Disc 1 - Track 11
Song Title: *"Seven Fat Cows"*

Joseph Becomes a Leader

Fingerplay

Do the fingerplay *"Joseph's Brothers"*. Focus on the sound and motion for the letter 'E'.

<u>Key Idea</u>: 'E' = pretend to shake an empty jar upside down and say *E-E*

Bible Story

Read the Bible story from **one** of the following resources:

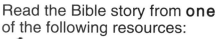 Scripture: Genesis 48:10-11, 15-16

 *The New Bible in Pictures for Little Eyes* p. 76-77

<u>Key Idea</u>: Jacob blessed Joseph's sons.

Active Exploration

Ask students if they have any relatives that live far away. Ask students if they have had someone they love pass away. Say, *Pictures help us remember those we love.* Have students look at or share pictures of their relatives. Discuss special things about the people in the pictures.

<u>Key Idea</u>: Joseph hadn't seen his father for a long time. He had to keep the memories of his father in his mind until he saw him again.

Letter Activity

Use the 'E' flashcard from the Appendix. Have students trace the capital and small letter 'E's" on the flashcard with their fingers. Using the flashcard as a model, choose either a bar of soap on a mirror or an ice cube on construction paper to write more 'E's'.

<u>Key Idea</u>: Practice the motions needed to make the letter 'E'.

Bible Activity

Bless your students. Have them take turns kneeling down. Lay your hands on their heads and pray for God to take care of them and help them to do what He asks of them.

Explain to students that God has a special purpose for each of them. There is a reason He created each one of them.

<u>Key Idea</u>: Jacob passed God's blessing on to Joseph's sons.

Corresponding Music

None for this lesson

Young Moses

Fingerplay

Do the fingerplay *"Baby in the Basket"*. Focus on the sound and motion for the letter 'F'.

Key Idea: 'F' = wiggle 10 fingers up like flames and say *F-F*

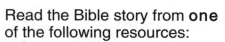
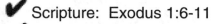

Bible Story

Read the Bible story from **one** of the following resources:

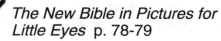

✔ Scripture: Exodus 1:6-11

✔ *A Child's First Bible* p. 40-41

✔ *The New Bible in Pictures for Little Eyes* p. 78-79

Key Idea: Israel's people cried out.

Math Activity

Youngers: Use motions from the following list for students to perform in order to "make" bricks: dig, stir, pound, shape, or lift. Use words such as *few, many, once,* or *more than once* to explain how many times to do a motion (i.e. Say, *Dig once*).
Olders: Command students to use a certain number of blocks to build the following types of towers: tall, wide, flat, and short. Tell how the towers are alike or different.

Key Idea: The people of Israel worked hard as slaves in Egypt.

Letter Activity

Copy the 'F' flashcard found in the Appendix. Show the letter side of the flashcard to the students. Read the *Hint* aloud. Demonstrate the motion and sound for 'F'. Have the students repeat it.

Key Idea: Students should eventually do the motion and say the sound for each flashcard without needing a *Hint* or a demonstration from you.

Bible Activity

Copy *Count on Me* (in Appendix). Direct students to draw bricks by making a brown rectangle in the boxes. Younger students make 1 brick in each box. Older students make 2 bricks in each box. Point to each brick as you count it with the students. Write the numbers on the lines below each box as you count. Say the numbers below the boxes to count by 1's or by 2's (counting either '1', '2', '3'... or '2', '4', '6' ...).

Key Idea: The people of Israel were forced to make bricks and to build for the Egyptians.

Corresponding Music

None this lesson

Fingerplay: Baby in the Basket
(Sung to the tune of *"Skip to My Lou"*)

Days 1-5

Baby in the basket	*Arms rock a baby*
Float, float, float	*Wiggle fingers back and forth*
Baby in the basket	*Arms rock a baby*
Float, float, float	*Wiggle fingers back and forth*
Baby in the basket	*Arms rock a baby*
Float, float, float	*Wiggle fingers back and forth*
God saved Moses	*Point up*
We all know.	*Point to brain*

Moses saw God's fire	*Shield eyes with hand*
F... F... F...	*Wiggle 10 fingers like flames*
Moses saw God's fire	*Shield eyes with hand*
F... F... F...	*Wiggle 10 fingers like flames*
Moses saw God's fire	*Shield eyes with hand*
F... F... F...	*Wiggle 10 fingers like flames*
God spoke to Moses	*Point up*
From the bush.	*Cup hands around mouth*

God wants Israel set	*Point up*
Free, free, free	*Wrists together, pull apart*
God wants Israel set	*Point up*
Free, free, free	*Wrists together, pull apart*
God wants Israel set	*Point up*
Free, free, free	*Wrists together, pull apart*
Israel has cried	*Rub eyes*
Out to Me.	*Point up*

Young Moses

Fingerplay

Do the fingerplay *"Baby in the Basket"*. Focus on the sound and motion for the letter 'F'.

Key Idea: 'F' = wiggle 10 fingers up like flames and say *F-F*

Letter Activity

Use masking tape to make a large 'F' on the floor. Have students place blocks on the tape to trace the letter. Each time a block is placed on the tape, students make the letter **sound**.

Key Idea: Each letter has a name and a sound, just like animals do. For example, a lamb may be named Whitey, but it makes the sound, *Baaa*.

Bible Story

Read the Bible story from **one** of the following resources:

✔ Scripture: Exodus 1:22, 2:1-4

✔ *A Child's First Bible* p. 36

✔ *The New Bible in Pictures for Little Eyes* p. 80-81

Key Idea: God saved baby Moses.

Bible Activity

Act out the Bible story. Give students the following directions: *Pretend to weave a basket with your hands. Pick up an imaginary baby, rock it, kiss it, and place it in the basket. Cover the baby up. Look around to make sure no one is watching. Carry the basket and tiptoe to the river. Kneel down and set the basket in the water. Fold your hands and pray. Ask God to watch over the baby.* Ask students, *Do you think your parents pray for God to watch over you? Why?*

Key Idea: God watched over Moses. God is always watching over us too.

Art Activity

Instruct students to cut **green paper** into strips of various sizes. Tell students to **glue** the strips on **blue construction paper** to show grass and water. Have students cut an oval shape out of **brown paper** to be a basket and glue it "hidden" behind the green grass strips.

Key Idea: Moses' mother saved him by hiding him in a basket by the water. She trusted God to take care of him.

Corresponding Music

The Singing Bible, Disc 1 - Track 12 Song Title: *"Baby Moses"*

Young Moses

Fingerplay

Do the fingerplay *"Baby in the Basket"*. Focus on the sound and motion for the letter 'F'.

<u>Key Idea</u>: 'F' = wiggle 10 fingers up like flames and say *F-F*

Letter Activity

Write a big 'F' on a piece of paper. Have students use fingerpaints, paints and paintbrushes, or playdough to fill in the letter.

<u>Key Idea</u>: Students will become familiar with the shape and appearance of the capital letter 'F'.

Bible Story

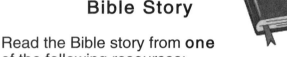

Read the Bible story from **one** of the following resources:

✔ Scripture: Exodus 2:5-10

✔ *A Child's First Bible* p. 37

✔ *The New Bible in Pictures for Little Eyes* p. 82-83

<u>Key Idea</u>: Moses was saved.

Dramatic Play

Have students practice taking care of a baby stuffed animal or doll by doing the following actions: Diaper the "baby" by taping on a paper towel. Feed the baby with a spoon or bottle. Burp the baby using a burp cloth. Rock the baby, while singing *Jesus Loves Me*. Have the baby "play" with a few toys. Tuck the baby into bed with a blanket. Give the baby a goodnight kiss.

<u>Key Idea</u>: God made sure the king's daughter found Moses, so Moses was safe.

Bible Activity

Act out the Bible story. Have students pretend to be the king's daughter walking along the river. Give the students the following directions:

Shade your eyes and point to the river. Push aside the reeds, lean down, and reach for the basket. Open the basket and look surprised. Say, "A baby!" Pick up the baby and pat it. Say, "Can you find someone to take care of this baby? I want to keep him." Ask students, What are some ways your mother takes care of you?

<u>Key Idea</u>: Moses' sister was watching. She ran to get her mother to take care of Moses for the king's daughter.

Corresponding Music

The Singing Bible, Disc 1 - Track 12
Song Title: *"Baby Moses"*

Young Moses

Fingerplay

Do the fingerplay *"Baby in the Basket".* Focus on the sound and motion for the letter 'F'.

<u>Key Idea</u>: 'F' = wiggle 10 fingers up like flames and say *F-F*

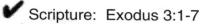

Bible Story

Read the Bible story from **one** of the following resources:

✔ Scripture: Exodus 3:1-7
✔ *A Child's First Bible* p. 38-39
✔ *The New Bible in Pictures for Little Eyes* p. 84-85

<u>Key Idea</u>: God spoke to Moses.

Devotional Activity

Read and discuss the devotion from **one** of the following resources:

✔ *Big Thoughts for Little People*
Read the two pages for letter 'F'.

✔ *Teach Them to Your Children*
Read the two pages for letter 'F'.

✔ *My ABC Bible Verses*
Read the two pages for letter 'F'.

<u>Key Idea</u>: <u>Key Idea</u>: Share a devotional focusing on character traits or memory work based on the letter 'F'.

Letter Activity

Copy the *Hide and Seek 'F'* page. Have students circle, color, highlight, or point to the 'F's' on the page. Younger students may need help in order to find any 'F's' at all. It is not necessary to find all the 'F's'. On the bottom of the page, have students connect 'F' to 'f' by tracing the dotted line from left to right.

<u>Key Idea</u>: Students should eventually recognize the capital and small letter 'F' within words.

Bible Activity

Copy the *Number Seven* page. Have students find seven shoes in a magazine or catalog to cut out. Use a marker to circle, box, or outline each shoe so that students have a line to follow as they cut. Have students glue the shoes on the *Number Seven* page. Save this page. A page will be added each week to make a counting book.

<u>Key Idea</u>: God spoke to Moses from a burning bush. Moses took off his shoes to show the place was holy.

Corresponding Music

The Singing Bible, Disc 1 - Track 13
Song Titles: *"Pharaoh Told Them No"*

Hide and Seek 'F'

Baby in the basket

Float, float, float

Baby in the basket

Float, float, float

Number
Seven

7

Young Moses

Fingerplay

Do the fingerplay *"Baby in the Basket"*. Focus on the sound and motion for the letter 'F'.

<u>Key Idea</u>: 'F' = wiggle 10 fingers up like flames and say *F-F*

Bible Story

Read the Bible story from **one** of the following resources:

✔ Scripture: Exodus 7:1-5, 17

✔ *A Child's First Bible* p. 42-43 (plus the Scripture listed above)

✔ *The New Bible in Pictures for Little Eyes* p. 86-87

<u>Key Idea</u>: Moses warned the king.

Active Exploration

Put warm, soapy water in a sink or dishtub, along with some of the following items: measuring spoons and cups, ladles, wire whisks, egg beaters, strainers, basters or medicine droppers, and funnels. Have students "explore" the water. At the end, add red food coloring like the water turned to blood. Ask, *Would you want to drink this water?*

<u>Key Idea</u>: God turned the Nile River to blood because the king wouldn't let the Israelites go.

Letter Activity

Use the 'F' flashcard from the Appendix. Have students trace the capital and small letter 'F's' on the flashcard with their fingers. Using the flashcard as a model, choose either sidewalk chalk or 2 crayons taped together and paper to write more 'F's'.

<u>Key Idea</u>: Practice the motions needed to make the letter 'F'.

Bible Activity

Have the following discussion with the students: *Have you ever gotten into trouble for not listening to your parents? What are some things that are "no-no's" at your house? Did the king get into trouble because he didn't listen to Moses' and Aaron's warning? Let's pray and ask God to help us listen to our parents' warnings, so we don't get hurt.*

<u>Key Idea</u>: It is better to listen to a warning the first time, rather than not to listen and suffer the consequences.

Corresponding Music

The Singing Bible, Disc 1 - Track 13
Song Titles: *"Pharaoh Told Them No"*

The Exodus

Fingerplay

Do the fingerplay *"Let My People Go"*. Focus on the sound and motion for the letter 'G'.

<u>Key Idea</u>: 'G' = hold nose, wave other hand in the air, and say *G-G*

Letter Activity

Copy the 'G' flashcard found in the Appendix. Show the letter side of the flashcard to the students. Read the *Hint* aloud. Demonstrate the motion and sound for 'G'. Have the students repeat it.

<u>Key Idea</u>: Students should eventually do the motion and say the sound for each flashcard without needing a *Hint* or a demonstration.

Bible Story

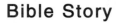 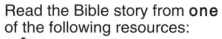 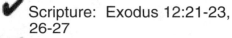 

Read the Bible story from **one** of the following resources:

✔ Scripture: Exodus 12:21-23, 26-27

✔ *A Child's First Bible* p. 44

✔ *The New Bible in Pictures for Little Eyes* p. 88-89

<u>Key Idea</u>: God sent the last plague.

Bible Activity

Copy *Count on Me* (in Appendix). Direct students to draw doors by making a brown rectangle with a doorknob in the boxes. Younger students make 1 door in each box. Older students make 2 doors in each box. Point to each door as you count it with the students. Write the numbers on the lines below each box as you count. Say the numbers below the boxes to count by 1's or by 2's (counting either '1', '2', '3'... or '2', '4', '6' ...).

<u>Key Idea</u>: The Israelites marked their doors with blood, so the angel of the Lord would pass over them.

Math Activity

<u>Youngers</u>: Line up 3 toys. Ask, *Which toy is first? Next? Last?* Have students change the order of the toys and tell you where each toy is placed each time.
<u>Olders</u>: Line up 5 or more toys. Discuss which toys are first, second, third, and so on. Give directions for changing the order of the toys. For example, *Put the lion first.*

<u>Key Idea</u>: The firstborn, or oldest, child in each Egyptian family died.

Corresponding Music

The Singing Bible, Disc 1 - Track 14
Song Title: *"The Exodus"*

Fingerplay: Let My People Go

Days 1-5

God said,	*Point up*
Let my people go!	*Wrists together, pull apart*
Pharaoh kept on saying, *No!*	*Shake head, "No"*
Pharaoh's sad.	*Rub eyes*
His son is dead.	*Lay down*
Let my people go,	*Wrists together, pull apart*
God said.	*Point up*
God said,	*Point up*
Let my people go!	*Wrists together, pull apart*
They walked	*Pat legs with hands*
To where the Red Sea flows.	*Wiggle fingers back and forth*
G... G...	*Hold nose, put hand up*
Pharaoh chased them as they fled.	*Pat legs faster with hands*
Let my people go,	*Wrists together, pull apart*
God said.	*Point up*
God said,	*Point up*
Let my people go!	*Wrists together, pull apart*
The waters of the sea God blows.	*Blow with cheeks out*
G... G...	*Hold nose, put hand up*
Pharaoh's army's dead.	*Lay down on ground*
Let my people go,	*Wrists together, pull apart*
God said.	*Point up*

The Exodus

Fingerplay

Do the fingerplay *"Let My People Go"*. Focus on the sound and motion for the letter 'G'.

<u>Key Idea</u>: 'G' = hold nose, wave other hand in the air, and say *G-G*

Bible Story

Read the Bible story from **one** of the following resources:

✔ Scripture: Exodus 12:29-33
✔ *A Child's First Bible* p. 45
✔ *The New Bible in Pictures for Little Eyes* p. 90-91

<u>Key Idea</u>:   The king was sorry.

Devotional Activity

Read and discuss the devotion from **one** of the following resources:

✔ *Big Thoughts for Little People*
   Read the two pages for letter 'G'.

✔ *Teach Them to Your Children*
   Read the two pages for letter 'G'.

✔ *My ABC Bible Verses*
   Read the two pages for letter 'G'.

<u>Key Idea</u>:   Share a devotional focusing on character traits or memory work based on the letter 'G'.

Letter Activity

Write a big 'G' on a piece of paper. Have students glue cotton balls or pieces of yarn to the letter. Younger students will need you to apply drops of glue on the letter for them first.

<u>Key Idea</u>:   Students will become familiar with the shape and appearance of the capital letter 'G'.

Bible Activity

Act out the Bible story. Give students the following directions: *Lay a stuffed animal on the floor. Kneel over it and say, "He's dead". Rub your eyes and make crying sounds. Motion to Moses to come. Point your arm out and say, "Go! I should have listened to your God". Lean over the stuffed animal, as if you are weeping.*

<u>Key Idea</u>:   The king did not listen to God until the 10th plague killed his son. Do you listen to God's word, the Bible?

Corresponding Music

The Singing Bible, Disc 1 - Track 14
Song Title: *"The Exodus"*

The Exodus

Fingerplay

Do the fingerplay *"Let My People Go"*. Focus on the sound and motion for the letter 'G'.

Key Idea: 'G' = hold nose, wave other hand in the air, and say *G-G*

Bible Story

Read the Bible story from **one** of the following resources:

 Scripture: Exodus 13:18, 21-22

 The New Bible in Pictures for Little Eyes p. 92-93

Key Idea: God led his people.

Active Exploration

Play *"Follow the Leader"*. Say, *Let's pretend we are going on a trip just like the Israelites. Listen to my directions, so you know where to go.* Give movement directions with positional words in them. See the following examples for ideas: Tiptoe through the room. Step over the toy. Hop around the chair. Spin in front of the door. Crawl under the table. Stomp past the doorway. March on the rug. Reach up to the ceiling.

Key Idea: God led the Israelites with a cloud all day and night.

Letter Activity

Copy the *Hide and Seek 'G'* page. Have students circle, color, highlight, or point to the 'G's' on the page. Younger students may need help finding any 'G's' at all. It is not necessary to find all the 'G's'. On the bottom of the page, have students connect 'G' to 'g' by tracing the dotted line from left to right.

Key Idea: Students should eventually recognize the capital and small letter 'G' within words.

Bible Activity

Copy the *Number Eight* page. Have students find eight pieces of jewelry in a magazine or catalog to cut out. Use a marker to circle, box, or outline each piece of jewelry so that students have a line to follow as they cut. Have students glue the jewelry on the *Number Eight* page. Save this page. A page will be added each week to make a '1-10' counting book.

Key Idea: As the Israelites left Egypt, they were given jewelry and other gifts.

Corresponding Music

The Singing Bible, Disc 2 - Track 1
Song Title: *"The Red Sea"*

Hide and Seek 'G'

God said,

Let my people go!

They walked

To where the Red Sea flows.

G... G... G...

G ---------------------------------- g

G ---------------------------------- g

Number Eight

8

The Exodus

Fingerplay

Do the fingerplay "*Let My People Go*". Focus on the sound and motion for the letter 'G'.

Key Idea: 'G' = hold nose, wave other hand in the air, and say *G-G*

Bible Story

Read the Bible story from **one** of the following resources:

✔ Scripture: Exodus 14:21-27

✔ *A Child's First Bible* p. 46-47

✔ *The New Bible in Pictures for Little Eyes* p. 94-97

Key Idea: God parted the Red Sea.

Art Activity

Help students put **strips of masking tape** vertically down the center of **shiny, white painting paper.** Older students may use **crayons** to draw and color fish on the paper. All students should paint the entire paper with **watercolors** in blues, greens, and purples to represent the sea. Last, remove the tape to see a "path" through the sea.

Key Idea: God parted the Red Sea, and the Israelites crossed on dry ground.

Letter Activity

Use masking tape to make a large 'G' on the floor. Have students drive a toy car or other toy vehicle on the tape to trace the letter. Have students say the letter **sound** as they drive.

Key Idea: Each letter has a name and a sound, just like animals do. For example, a bird may be named Robin, but it makes the sound, *Chirp.*

Bible Activity

Have students choose props to set up a scene that represents the Red Sea crossing.

Ask students to choose a prop for each of the following things: Moses, the Egyptians, the Israelites, a staff, a path, and the sea. Students may also act out the story after setting up the scene.

Key Idea: God saved the Israelites as they fled from the Egyptians, but the king's army drowned.

Corresponding Music

The Singing Bible, Disc 2 - Track 1
Song Title: *"The Red Sea"*

The Exodus

Fingerplay

Do the fingerplay *"Let My People Go"*. Focus on the sound and motion for the letter 'G'.

Key Idea: 'G' = hold nose, wave other hand in the air, and say *G-G*

Bible Story

Read the Bible story from **one** of the following resources:

✔ Scripture: Exodus 16:11-15, 17:5-6

✔ *A Child's First Bible* p. 48-51

✔ *The New Bible in Pictures for Little Eyes* p. 98-101

Key Idea: God gave the people of Israel food and water.

Dramatic Play

Scatter "manna" on the floor. Some ideas for manna include the following: cotton balls, torn bread, torn paper towels, or dry pasta. Set a basket at one end of the room. Have students pick up one piece of manna at a time, run over, and put it in the basket. Direct older students to gather and count an assigned number of pieces.

Key Idea: God provided manna from above and water from a rock.

Letter Activity

Use the 'G' flashcard from the Appendix. Have students trace the capital and small letter 'G' on the flashcard with their fingers. Using the flashcard as a model, give students either a small amount of cooking oil or liquid soap on an aluminum pan or plate to use to write more 'G's'.

Key Idea: Practice the motions needed to make the letter 'G'.

Bible Activity

Have students name some of their favorite things to drink. Then, have students name a few of their favorite foods.

Ask students to imagine what it would be like to eat the same thing every day. Point out that even then, God says we should be thankful. Say, *Let's remember not to complain about the many foods and drinks we have. Let's thank God for those foods right now.* Pray with the students.

Key Idea: The Israelites were worried about having food and water, but God made sure they had enough.

Corresponding Music

None this lesson

God's Laws

Fingerplay

Do the fingerplay *"Two Helping Hands"*. Focus on the sound and motion for the letter 'H'.

Key Idea: 'H' = lace fingers, move hands up and down, and say *H-H*

Letter Activity

Copy the 'H' flashcard found in the Appendix. Show the letter side of the flashcard to the students. Read the *Hint* aloud. Demonstrate the motion and sound for 'H'. Have the students repeat it.

Key Idea: Students should eventually do the motion and say the sound for each flashcard without needing a *Hint* or a demonstration from you.

Bible Story

Read the Bible story from **one** of the following resources:

 Scripture: Exodus 31:18, 32:15-16
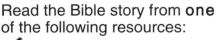 *A Child's First Bible* p. 54-55
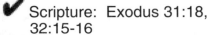 *The New Bible in Pictures for Little Eyes* p. 102-103

Key Idea: The Ten Commandments

Bible Activity

Copy *Count on Me* (in Appendix). Direct students to draw stones by making a grey oval in the boxes. Younger students make 1 stone in each box. Older students make 2 stones in each box. Point to each stone as you count it with the students. Write the numbers on the lines below each box as you count. Say the numbers below the boxes to count by 1's or by 2's (counting either '1', '2', '3'... or '2', '4', '6' ...).

Key Idea: On Mt. Sinai, God gave Moses 2 stone tablets with 10 Commandments for Israel to follow.

Math Activity

Youngers: Give students a large sheet of paper. Let them apply stamps or stickers all over the paper. Help them count the stamps or stickers and circle groups of 1-10.
Olders: Use sheets of paper to make a 10 page booklet. Number the pages 1-10. Let students apply the matching number of stamps or stickers for each page.

Key Idea: God gave Moses and Israel 10 Commandments.

Corresponding Music

The Singing Bible, Disc 2 - Track 2
Song Title: *"Ten Commandments"*

Fingerplay: Two Helping Hands

Days 1-5

Two helping hands	*Lace fingers, move up and down*
Carry 10 Commandments.	*Hold up 10 fingers*
H... H... H...	*Lace fingers, move up and down*
God shows his people	*Point up*
He is there with us.	*Pat on back*

Two helping hands	*Lace fingers, move up and down*
Carry gifts for God's house.	*Cup hands and hold out*
H... H... H...	*Lace fingers, move up and down*
God shows his people	*Point up*
He is there with us.	*Pat on back*

Two helping hands	*Lace fingers, move up and down*
Work to build God's house.	*Tap fist on top of other fist*
H... H... H...	*Lace fingers, move up and down*
God shows his people	*Point up*
He is there with us.	*Pat on back*

Two helping hands	*Lace fingers, move up and down*
Fold in thankfulness.	*Fold hands*
H... H... H...	*Lace fingers, move up and down*
God shows his people	*Point up*
He is there with us.	*Pat on back*

God's Laws

Fingerplay

Do the fingerplay *"Two Helping Hands"*. Focus on the sound and motion for the letter 'H'.

<u>Key Idea</u>: 'H' = lace fingers, move hands up and down, and say *H-H*

Bible Story

Read the Bible story from **one** of the following resources:

✔ Scripture: Exodus 32:7-8,19
✔ *A Child's First Bible* p. 56-57
✔ *The New Bible in Pictures for Little Eyes* p. 104-107

<u>Key Idea</u>: The people prayed to a golden calf.

Devotional Activity

Read and discuss the devotion from **one** of the following resources:

✔ *Big Thoughts for Little People*
Read the two pages for letter 'H'.

✔ *Teach Them to Your Children*
Read the two pages for letter 'H'.

✔ *My ABC Bible Verses*
Read the two pages for letter 'H'.

<u>Key Idea</u>: Share a devotional focusing on character traits or memory work based on the letter 'H'.

Letter Activity

Write a big 'H' on a piece of paper. Have students glue dried macaroni or raisins to the letter. Younger students will need you to apply drops of glue on the letter for them first.

<u>Key Idea</u>: Students will become familiar with the shape and appearance of the capital letter 'H'.

Bible Activity

Say, *It is important for us to know who we are praying to when we say our prayers. We are not praying to an object, we are praying to the one and only God.* Model the following ways to show how to pray to God: fold hands, kneel or sit quietly, do not look at other things during prayer, do not move around, and do not speak in a silly voice. Say, *Let's pray now and thank the one and only God for creating all of us.*

<u>Key Idea</u>: God is very special. He is the one and only God. We should pray only to him.

Corresponding Music

The Singing Bible, Disc 2 - Track 2
Song Title: *"Ten Commandments"*

God's Laws

Fingerplay

Do the fingerplay *"Two Helping Hands"*. Focus on the sound and motion for the letter 'H'.

Key Idea: 'H' = lace fingers, move hands up and down, and say *H-H*

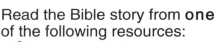

Bible Story

Read the Bible story from **one** of the following resources:

✔ Scripture: Exodus 35:4-9

✔ *A Child's First Bible* p. 58-59

✔ *The New Bible in Pictures for Little Eyes* p. 108-109

Key Idea: God's people brought gifts for the tabernacle.

Active Exploration

Have students build a small example of God's tabernacle. Wrap 5 duplos or blocks in tin foil for pillars. Drape a small dark towel or napkin over the pillars. Older students may lay small bits of colored napkin or wrapping paper in the "tabernacle" to be gifts of cloth. Students may also put a few coins in the tabernacle and spray perfume in the air over it to show those gifts too.

Key Idea: The Israelites brought gifts to build God's tabernacle.

Letter Activity

Copy the *Hide and Seek 'H'* page. Have students circle, color, highlight, or point to the 'H's' on the page. Younger students may need help in order to find any 'H's' at all. It is not necessary to find all the 'H's'. On the bottom of the page, have students connect 'H' to 'h' by tracing the dotted line from left to right.

Key Idea: Students should eventually recognize the capital and small letter 'H' within words.

Bible Activity

Copy the *Number Nine* page. Have students find nine bottles of perfume or pieces of pretty cloth in a magazine or catalog to cut out. Use a marker to circle, box, or outline the perfume or cloth so that students have a line to follow as they cut. Have students glue the perfume bottles or cloth pieces on the *Number Nine* page. Save this page. A page will be added each week to make a '1-10' counting book.

Key Idea: God's people brought perfume and cloth as gifts to God.

Corresponding Music

The Singing Bible, Disc 2 - Track 2
Song Title: *"Ten Commandments"*

Hide and Seek 'H'

Two helping hands

Carry gifts for God's house.

H... H... H...

God shows his people

He is there with us.

H ------------------------------- h

H ------------------------------- h

Number Nine

9

God's Laws

Fingerplay

Do the fingerplay *"Two Helping Hands"*. Focus on the sound and motion for the letter 'H'.

<u>Key Idea</u>: 'H' = lace fingers, move hands up and down, and say *H-H*

Bible Story

Read the Bible story from **one** of the following resources:

 Scripture: Exodus 40:36-38

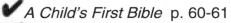 *A Child's First Bible* p. 60-61

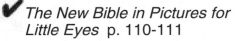 *The New Bible in Pictures for Little Eyes* p. 110-111

<u>Key Idea</u>: God watched over the tabernacle.

Dramatic Play

Put a blanket over a table or 2 chairs to represent an Israelite tent. Turn off the lights, as if it is night. Shine a flashlight to represent God's fire. When you move the "fire" away, have students take down the tent and follow the fire to the spot where it stops. Then, have students put up the tent at that new spot. Repeat the exercise several times.

<u>Key Idea</u>: God watches over us today, just like He watched over the Israelites.

Letter Activity

Use the 'H' flashcard from the Appendix. Have students trace the capital and small letter 'H' on the flashcard with their fingers. Using the flashcard as a model, choose either pudding, chocolate syrup, baby food, or fingerpaint on a plate, pan, or piece of paper for students to write more 'H's'.

<u>Key Idea</u>: Practice the motions needed to make the letter 'H'.

Bible Activity

Say, *God had the Israelites build him a beautiful tabernacle to be his "house". Your church is God's house too.* Have students describe some of the beautiful things in their church.

Say, *We have those beautiful things in God's house to show God how special He is to us.*

<u>Key Idea</u>: The church is God's house today, just like the tabernacle was God's house in Bible times.

Corresponding Music

The Singing Bible, Disc 2 - Track 2
Song Title: *"Ten Commandments"*

God's Laws

Fingerplay

Do the fingerplay *"Two Helping Hands"*. Focus on the sound and motion for the letter 'H'.

Key Idea: 'H' = lace fingers, move hands up and down, and say *H-H*

Bible Story

Read the Bible story from **one** of the following resources:

✔ Scripture: Numbers 13:27-28, 30-31

✔ *A Child's First Bible* p. 62-63

✔ *The New Bible in Pictures for Little Eyes* p. 112-113

Key Idea: The people were afraid.

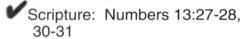

Art Activity

Use **brown crayons** to draw grape branches on **green construction paper**. Have students glue **cotton balls** or **'O'-shaped cereal** in clusters like grapes on branches. For younger students apply drops of glue for them. You may choose to have older students **fingerpaint** to make the grapes instead.

Key Idea: The land of Canaan was full of large fruit and other good things.

Letter Activity

Use masking tape to make a large 'H' on the floor. Have students tiptoe on the tape to trace the letter. Then, have students jump off the end of the letter saying the letter **sound** as they jump.

Key Idea: Each letter has a name and a sound, just like animals do. For example, a duck may be named Ducky, but it makes the sound, *Quack*.

Bible Activity

Have students pretend to be spies that Moses sent to Canaan. Tell students to tiptoe and sneak around. Have them pretend to pick very large grapes, carry them on their shoulders, and sneak very slowly out of the city. Have them look scared and point up to show how tall the men in Canaan are. Tell students to shake their heads and say, *No, we don't want to fight them!*

Key Idea: The Israelites forgot to trust God, so they were punished.

Corresponding Music

The Singing Bible, Disc 2 - Track 3
Song Title: *"Forty Years You'll Go"*

Joshua Leads Israel

Fingerplay

Do the fingerplay *"What Do You Know?"* Focus on reviewing the sounds and motions for the letters.

Key Idea: Practice the sounds and motions for the letters 'A-H'.

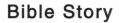

Bible Story

Read the Bible story from **one** of the following resources:

✔ Scripture: Numbers 27:15-20

✔ *The New Bible in Pictures for Little Eyes* p. 120-121, 124-125

Key Idea: Joshua led the Israelites.

Devotional Activity

Read and discuss the devotion from **one** of the following resources:

✔ *Big Thoughts for Little People*
Review verses for 'E', 'F', 'G', 'H'

✔ *Teach Them to Your Children*
Review verses for 'E', 'F', 'G', 'H'

✔ *My ABC Bible Verses*
Review verses for 'E', 'F', 'G', 'H'

Key Idea: Share a devotional focusing on character traits or memory work based on the letters 'E', 'F', 'G', 'H'.

Letter Activity

This is a review week. Review all the flashcards from the previous weeks. Show the letter side of each flashcard to the students. Have them respond with the motion and sound. If needed, read the *Hint* or demonstrate the motion and sound.

Key Idea: Students should eventually do the motion and say the sound for each flashcard without needing a *Hint* or a demonstration from you.

Bible Activity

Copy the *Number Ten* page. Have students find ten men in a magazine or catalog to cut out. Use a marker to circle, box, or outline each man so that students have a line to follow as they cut. Have students glue the men on the *Number Ten* page. Staple together the pages that you saved from the previous weeks to make a '1-10' counting book.

Key Idea: The Israelites wandered in the desert for 40 years, because they did not listen to God. Now, it was time to enter the Promised Land.

Corresponding Music

None this lesson

Fingerplay: What Do You Know?

Days 1-5

We've learned about *A-A-Adam*   *Hands on cheeks in surprise*

And *B-B-Boat,*   *Hug yourself and rock side-to-side*

C-C-Clippity clop   *Tap palms on thighs in rhythm*

And *D-D-Dusty* camel.   *Hold reins; move up and down*

E-E-Empty jars   *Shake hand to shake empty jar*

And *F-F-Fire,*   *Wiggle 10 fingers like flames*

G-G-Gurgle   *Hold nose, put hand up*

And *H-H-Helping* hands.   *Lace fingers, move up and down*

Now, as Joshua   *Marching motions with arms*

Marches around,   *Draw circles in the air*

God makes Jericho's   *Point up*

Walls fall down.   *Clap hands on the word, "down"*

Just like the others   *Open palms together like Bible*

God has plans for you too.   *Point up, then point to yourself*

Never forget   *Shake head, "No"*

What God can do!   *Spread arms wide*

Number
Ten

10

Joshua Leads Israel

Fingerplay

Do the fingerplay *"What Do You Know?"* Focus on reviewing the sounds and motions for the letters.

<u>Key Idea</u>: Practice the sounds and motions for the letters 'A-H'.

Letter Activity

Choose one or more of the letters 'A-H' to review. Use masking tape to make the large review letter on the floor. Have students sit on a pillow and scoot on the tape to trace the letter. Have students say the letter **sound** as they scoot.

<u>Key Idea</u>: Each letter has a name and a sound, just like animals do. For example, a frog may be named Slimy, but it makes the sound, *Ribbit.*

Bible Story

Read the Bible story from **one** of the following resources:

✔ Scripture: Joshua 2:2-6, 12-13

✔ *The New Bible in Pictures for Little Eyes* p. 130-131

<u>Key Idea</u>: Rahab helped the spies.

Bible Activity

Act out the Bible story. Use props for the branches and the rope. You are Rahab, and the students are the spies.

Have the spies tiptoe into the city and knock on your door. Then, tell the spies to lay down and hide. Cover them up with "branches". Next, have the spies "climb down" a "rope" and sneak away. Leave the rope as a reminder of the spies' promise.

<u>Key Idea</u>: Rahab helped the spies, and God saved her and her family.

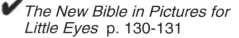

Art Activity

Give each student a **plastic knife** or a **butter knife**, **peanut butter** on a **plate**, a piece of **waxed paper**, and a handful of square or rectangular **crackers.** Tell students to "build" the wall of Jericho on their waxed paper using crackers and peanut butter. Show them how to spread peanut butter on the crackers to make them stick together. Students may break the crackers apart, if needed. A small piece of red yarn or licorice can be used for Rahab's rope.

<u>Key Idea</u>: The wall around Jericho was strong, but God is stronger.

Corresponding Music

The Singing Bible, Disc 2 - Track 5
Song Title: *"March Around Jericho"*

Joshua Leads Israel

Unit 10 - Day 3

Fingerplay

Do the fingerplay *"What Do You Know?"* Focus on reviewing the sounds and motions for the letters.

<u>Key Idea</u>: Practice the sounds and motions for the letters 'A-H'.

Bible Story

Read the Bible story from **one** of the following resources:

✔ Scripture: Joshua 3:7-8, 13, 17

✔ *A Child's First Bible* p. 68-69

✔ *The New Bible in Pictures for Little Eyes* p. 132-133

<u>Key Idea</u>: God made a path through the river.

Dramatic Play

Stick one long, straight piece of masking tape to the floor for the path through the river. Have students use a napkin, drink coaster, or bean bag for the "ark". As students walk on the "path", they balance the ark on their shoulders, hands, or heads. Tell students to try not to let the ark fall, because it was so special that it was never to touch the ground.

<u>Key Idea</u>: God made a path through the river, so the Israelites could get to the Promised Land.

Letter Activity

Choose one letter from 'A-H' to review. Write that letter on a big piece of paper. Use water to thin glue, and have students "paint" the glue on the letter. Then, sprinkle either salt, coffee grounds, glitter, or any kind of spice on the glue. Younger students will need you to help them with the sprinkling part.

<u>Key Idea</u>: Students will become familiar with the shape and appearance of the capital letters.

Bible Activity

Talk with students about things that God does for them. Possible examples include the following: healing them when they are sick, watching over them and keeping them safe, answering prayers that others pray for them, answering prayers they pray, forgiving them when they sin, loving them even though they are sinners, and sending Jesus to die for their sins.

<u>Key Idea</u>: God watches over us and does things for us every day, just like He helped the Israelites.

Corresponding Music

The Singing Bible, Disc 2 - Track 4
Song Title: *"Should They Build a Boat?"*

Joshua Leads Israel

Fingerplay

Do the fingerplay *"What Do You Know?"* Focus on reviewing the sounds and motions for the letters.

<u>Key Idea</u>: Practice the sounds and motions for the letters 'A-H'.

Bible Story

Read the Bible story from **one** of the following resources:

✔ Scripture: Joshua 6:1-5

✔ *A Child's First Bible* p. 70-71

✔ *The New Bible in Pictures for Little Eyes* p. 134-135

<u>Key Idea</u>: Jericho's walls fell down.

Math Activity

<u>Youngers</u>: Build a circle out of blocks. Have students duplicate the pattern with their own blocks. Lead students to march quietly around the block "wall" 7 times. Then, have students shout and knock the wall over. Continue the activity by building a triangular and a square wall as well. <u>Olders</u>: Do the above activity, using the following shapes instead: heart, rectangle, diamond, and pentagon.

<u>Key Idea</u>: God made the walls of Jericho fall down without a battle.

Letter Activity

Copy the *Hide-n-Seek Review* page. Choose a letter from 'E-H' for your students to review. Have students circle, color, highlight, or point to the chosen letter. Younger students may need help finding any of the chosen letters. On the bottom of the page, have students draw a line to connect each capital letter to its matching lowercase letter.

<u>Key Idea</u>: Students should eventually recognize the capital and small letters 'E-H' within words.

Bible Activity

Copy *Count on Me* (in Appendix). Direct students to draw horns by making a yellow triangle in each of the boxes. Younger students make 1 horn in each box. Older students make 2 horns in each box. Point to each horn as you count it. Write the numbers on the lines below each box as you count. Say the numbers below the boxes to count by 1's or by 2's (counting either '1', '2', '3' ... or '2', '4', '6' ...).

<u>Key Idea</u>: Israel did what God said.

Corresponding Music

The Singing Bible, Disc 2 - Track 5
Song Title: *"March Around Jericho"*

Hide and Seek Review

We've learned about E-E-Empty jars

And F-F-Fire,

G-G-Gurgle

And H-H-Helping hands.

E

F

G

H

f

e

h

g

Joshua Leads Israel

Fingerplay

Do the fingerplay *"What Do You Know?"* Focus on reviewing the sounds and motions for the letters.

Key Idea: Practice the sounds and motions for the letters 'A-H'.

Bible Story

Read the Bible story from **one** of the following resources:

✔ Scripture: Joshua 10:6-8, 13-14

✔ *A Child's First Bible* p. 72-73

✔ *The New Bible in Pictures for Little Eyes* p. 136-137

Key Idea: The sun didn't set.

Active Exploration

Explain that each hour in a day is made up of 60 minutes. Time 1 minute to show students how long it is. Talk about things that take about a minute to do, such as brushing teeth, making beds, and getting dressed. Have students clap, hop, or jog for 1 minute as you time them. Then, provide a snack and have students wait 1 minute to eat it.

Key Idea: Only God can add more minutes to a day, like He did for Joshua and the Israelites.

Letter Activity

Choose one or more of the flashcards from the previous weeks to review. Have students trace the capital and small letters on the flashcards with their fingers. Using the flashcards as models, choose either markers and markerboards or pieces of carpet and fingers to practice writing more letters.

Key Idea: Practice the motions needed to make the letters.

Bible Activity

Act out the Bible story. You are Joshua. Have the students use toys or stuffed animals to be the "soldiers" fighting.

Pray to the Lord to keep the sun from setting until the battle is over. Hold up your hands. Have the soldiers stop fighting and jump around saying, *Yeah! God made sure we won. The battle was his.*

Key Idea: God kept the sun shining longer to make sure the Israelites had time to beat their enemies.

Corresponding Music

None this lesson

The Time of the Judges

Fingerplay

Do the fingerplay *"Nothing's Impossible for God"*. Focus on the sound and motion for the letter 'I'.

<u>Key Idea</u>: 'I' = push palms up, as if lifting something heavy, and say *I-I*

Letter Activity

Copy the 'I' flashcard found in the Appendix. Show the letter side of the flashcard to the students. Read the *Hint* aloud. Demonstrate the motion and sound for 'I'. Have the students repeat it.

<u>Key Idea</u>: Students should eventually do the motion and say the sound for each flashcard without needing a *Hint* or a demonstration from you.

Bible Story

Read the Bible story from **one** of the following resources:
- Scripture: Judges 7:5-7
- *A Child's First Bible* p. 74-75
- *The New Bible in Pictures for Little Eyes* p. 138-139

<u>Key Idea</u>: God chose an army.

Bible Activity

Give each student a piece of paper. Help students complete each of the following directions one at a time: Draw a blue, wavy line at the bottom of the page to be a river. Draw a red smile on the left side of the page. Trace your hand on the right side of the page. Draw a circle around the tracing of your hand. Tell students, *We circled the hand to show that God chose the men who drank from their hands at the river.*

<u>Key Idea</u>: God used the way men drank at the river to help Gideon choose an army.

Active Exploration

<u>Youngers</u>: Have students look in a mirror and point to the following body parts as you name them: hair, eyes, eyebrows, nose, mouth, ears, stomach, fingers, knees, and toes.
<u>Olders</u>: Do the activity above, except have students name each body part as you point to it. Then, have them point to the following body parts: chin, shoulders, elbows, wrists, waist, and ankles.

<u>Key Idea</u>: God chose the men who used their hands to drink at the river.

Corresponding Music

The Singing Bible, Disc 2 - Track 6
Song Title: *"They Were Judges"*

Fingerplay: Nothing's Impossible for God

Days 1-5

Gideon,	*Hold hand to mouth, like a trumpet*
Samson,	*Show muscles*
And Ruth, too,	*Smile and point to smile*
Nothing's	*Shake head, "No"*
I-Impossible	*Push palms up, as if lifting*
For God to do.	*Point up*

A fighter,	*Hold hand to mouth, like a trumpet*
A strong man,	*Show muscles*
A kind woman, too,	*Smile and point to smile*
Nothing's	*Shake head, "No"*
I-Impossible	*Push palms up, as if lifting*
For God to do.	*Point up*

Hide and Seek 'I'

A fighter,

A strong man,

A kind woman, too.

Nothing's I-Impossible

For God to do.

The Time of the Judges

Fingerplay

Do the fingerplay *"Nothing's Impossible for God"*. Focus on the sound and motion for the letter 'I'.

Key Idea: 'I' = push palms up, as if lifting something heavy, and say *I-I*

Bible Story

Read the Bible story from **one** of the following resources:

✔ Scripture: Judges 16:2-3

✔ *A Child's First Bible* p. 76

✔ *The New Bible in Pictures for Little Eyes* p. 140-141

Key Idea: Samson was strong.

Math Activity

<u>Youngers</u>: Set out unopened cans and boxes of food or drink. Have students put the items in order from heaviest to lightest. Begin with 2 items and add more as needed.
<u>Olders</u>: Set out a variety of small items to "weigh" that could fit in a sock. Put each item in a separate sock. Have students lift the socks one at a time and order them from lightest to heaviest.

Key Idea: God gave Samson a special gift of strength.

Letter Activity

Copy the *Hide and Seek 'I'* page. Have students circle, color, highlight, or point to the 'I's' on the page. Younger students may need help in order to find any 'I's' at all. It is not necessary to find all the 'I's'. On the bottom of the page, have students connect 'I' to 'i' by tracing the dotted line from left to right.

Key Idea: Students should eventually recognize the capital and small letter 'I' within words.

Bible Activity

Copy *Count on Me* (in Appendix). Direct students to draw weights by making black colored circles in each of the boxes. Younger students make 2 weights in each box. Older students make 3 weights in each box. Point to each weight as you count. Write the numbers on the lines below each box as you count. Say the numbers below the boxes to count by 2's or by 3's (counting either '2', '4', '6'... or '3', '6', '9' ...).

Key Idea: God made Samson strong. He began to free Israel.

Corresponding Music

The Singing Bible, Disc 2 - Track 6
Song Title: *"They Were Judges"*

The Time of the Judges

Fingerplay

Do the fingerplay *"Nothing's Impossible for God"*. Focus on the sound and motion for the letter 'I'.

<u>Key Idea</u>: 'I' = push palms up, as if lifting something heavy, and say *I-I*

Bible Story

Read the Bible story from **one** of the following resources:

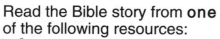 Scripture: Judges 16:17-19, 21-22, 28-30

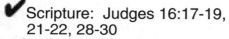 *A Child's First Bible* p. 77

✔ *The New Bible in Pictures for Little Eyes* p. 142-143

<u>Key Idea</u>: God gave Samson's strength back to him.

Dramatic Play

Have students build two tall pillars a large distance apart out of blocks. Have students stand between the two pillars. Give students balls or pairs of rolled up socks to toss at the pillars and knock them down. Have students rebuild the pillars and repeat the activity.

<u>Key Idea</u>: God gave Samson strength to pull down the "temple" of the Philistines and kill them.

Letter Activity

Write a big 'I' on a piece of paper. Have students glue dry 'O'-shaped cereal or dried beans to the letter. Younger students will need you to apply drops of glue on the letter for them first.

<u>Key Idea</u>: Students will become familiar with the shape and appearance of the capital letter 'I'.

Bible Activity

Say, *Samson forgot that his strength came from God. When Samson disobeyed God and let his hair be cut, God left him. What are some talents God has given you? Do you remember to thank God for those talents? Do you use your talents the way God wants you to use them?* Discuss some ways students could use their talents for God's glory. Say, *Let's thank God right now for our talents.* Lead students in prayer.

<u>Key Idea</u>: God has given each of us special talents, just like Samson. We need to use them for God's glory and not our own.

Corresponding Music

The Singing Bible, Disc 2 - Track 6
Song Title: *"They Were Judges"*

The Time of the Judges

Fingerplay

Do the fingerplay *"Nothing's Impossible for God"*. Focus on the sound and motion for the letter 'I'.

<u>Key Idea</u>: 'I' = push palms up, as if lifting something heavy, and say *I-I*

Letter Activity

Use the 'I' flashcard from the Appendix. Have students trace the capital and small letter 'I's" on the flashcard with their fingers. Using the flashcard as a model, choose either a bar of soap on a mirror or an ice cube on construction paper to write more 'I's'.

<u>Key Idea</u>: Practice the motions needed to make the letter 'I'.

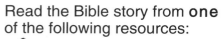

Bible Story

Read the Bible story from **one** of the following resources:

✔ Scripture: Ruth 1:15-18

✔ *A Child's First Bible* p. 80-81

✔ *The New Bible in Pictures for Little Eyes* p. 144-145

<u>Key Idea</u>: Ruth stayed with Naomi.

Bible Activity

Say, *Ruth stayed with Naomi and was a good daughter-in-law to her. God blessed Ruth for her kindness. How can you be a "good" son or daughter?*

Discuss some of the following examples: obey your parents, help at home, be kind to your brothers or sisters, share with others, and do what is asked of you without complaining

<u>Key Idea</u>: God blessed Ruth for her kindness to Naomi.

Devotional Activity

Read and discuss the devotion from **one** of the following resources:

✔ *Big Thoughts for Little People*
   Read the two pages for letter 'I'.

✔ *Teach Them to Your Children*
   Read the two pages for letter 'I'.

✔ *My ABC Bible Verses*
   Read the two pages for letter 'I'.

<u>Key Idea</u>: Share a devotional focusing on character traits or memory work based on the letter 'I'.

Corresponding Music

None this lesson

The Time of the Judges

Fingerplay

Do the fingerplay *"Nothing's Impossible for God"*. Focus on the sound and motion for the letter 'I'.

Key Idea: 'I' = push palms up, as if lifting something heavy, and say *I-I*

Bible Story

Read the Bible story from **one** of the following resources:

✔ Scripture: Ruth 2:2-7
✔ *The New Bible in Pictures for Little Eyes* p. 146-147

Key Idea: Ruth was a hard worker.

Art Activity

On **white paper** draw brown wheat stalks with a **crayon**. Have students **glue** on flakes of **cereal**, **popcorn seeds**, or grains of **rice** to be grains of wheat on the stalks.

Younger students will need you to apply drops of glue for them first.

Key Idea: Ruth picked up wheat in the field all day in the hot sun. God blessed her work.

Letter Activity

Use masking tape to make a large 'I' on the floor. Have students walk a stuffed animal on the tape to trace the letter. Then, have students walk the letter themselves, saying the letter **sound** as they walk.

Key Idea: Each letter has a name and a sound, just like animals do. For example, a lion may be named Leo, but it makes the sound, *Roar.*

Bible Activity

Say, *Ruth was a hard worker. How do you work hard to be a helper?*

Have students use a stuffed animal to pantomime some of the following examples of ways to help: wash dishes, make a bed, get dressed, brush teeth, comb hair, carry dishes to the sink, and put away toys.

Key Idea: God wants us to be hard workers to help others, just like Ruth worked hard to help Naomi.

Corresponding Music

None this lesson

Samuel Listens to God

Fingerplay

Do the fingerplay *"God Sends Samuel"*. Focus on the sound and motion for the letter 'J'.

<u>Key Idea</u>: 'J' = make 2 fingers jump on palm of hand and say *J-J*

Bible Story

Read the Bible story from **one** of the following resources:

✔ Scripture: 1 Samuel 1:10-11, 17

✔ *The New Bible in Pictures for Little Eyes* p. 148-149

<u>Key Idea</u>: Hannah asked God for a son.

Active Exploration

Have students look at pictures of themselves at special events such as holidays, birthday parties, or vacations from when they were younger. Talk about the people in the pictures and what events are taking place. Discuss what age the child was and any memories they might have of the event. Have students share things others have told them about their early years.

<u>Key Idea</u>: God gave Hannah a special baby. She was so thankful.

Letter Activity

Copy the 'J' flashcard found in the Appendix. Show the letter side of the flashcard to the students. Read the *Hint* aloud. Demonstrate the motion and sound for 'J'. Have the students repeat it.

<u>Key Idea</u>: Students should eventually do the motion and say the sound for each flashcard without needing a *Hint* or a demonstration from you.

Bible Activity

Copy *Count on Me* (in Appendix). Direct students to draw baby faces by making orange circles that each have 2 eyes and a mouth in the boxes. Younger students make 2 faces in each box. Older students make 3 faces in each box. Point to each face as you count it with the students. Write the numbers on the lines below each box as you count. Say the numbers below the boxes to count by 2's or by 3's (counting either '2', '4', '6'... or '3', '6', '9' ...).

<u>Key Idea</u>: Hannah promised God that if He gave her a baby, she would raise him to serve God.

Corresponding Music

None this lesson

Fingerplay: God Sends Samuel
(Sing to the tune of *"This Old Man"*)

Days 1-5

Sunday,	*Clap above head*
Monday,	*Clap in front of body*
Tuesday,	*Pat thighs with hands*
Wednesday,	*Pat floor with hands*
Thursday,	*Clap to the left*
Friday,	*Clap to the right*
Saturday,	*Roll hands forward*
Hannah's not *J-Joyful* today.	*2 fingers jump on palm of hand*
Asking God	*Fold hands*
For a baby someday.	*Rock arms, as if holding a baby*

Sunday,	*Clap above head*
Monday,	*Clap in front of body*
Tuesday,	*Pat thighs with hands*
Wednesday,	*Pat floor with hands*
Thursday,	*Clap to the left*
Friday,	*Clap to the right*
Saturday,	*Roll hands forward*
Hannah's *J-J-Joyful* today.	*2 fingers jump on palm of hand*
God has Samuel	*Point up*
On the way.	*Rock arms, as if holding a baby*

Sunday,	*Clap above head*
Monday,	*Clap in front of body*
Tuesday,	*Pat thighs with hands*
Wednesday,	*Pat floor with hands*
Thursday,	*Clap to the left*
Friday,	*Clap to the right*
Saturday,	*Roll hands forward*
Samuel listens to what God says,	*Cup hand to ear*
J-J-Joyfully	*2 fingers jump on palm of hand*
He does.	*Fold hands.*

Samuel Listens to God

Fingerplay

Do the fingerplay *"God Sends Samuel"*. Focus on the sound and motion for the letter 'J'.

Key Idea: 'J' = make 2 fingers jump on palm of hand and say *J-J*

Bible Story

Read the Bible story from **one** of the following resources:

 Scripture: 1 Samuel 2:26-28

✔ *The New Bible in Pictures for Little Eyes* p. 150-151

Key Idea: Hannah's prayer was answered.

Devotional Activity

Read and discuss the devotion from **one** of the following resources:

✔ *Big Thoughts for Little People*
Read the two pages for letter 'J'.

✔ *Teach Them to Your Children*
Read the two pages for letter 'J'.

✔ *My ABC Bible Verses*
Read the two pages for letter 'J'.

Key Idea: Share a devotional focusing on character traits or memory work based on the letter 'J'.

Letter Activity

Write a big 'J' on a piece of paper. Have students use fingerpaints, paints and paintbrushes, or playdough to fill in the letter.

Key Idea: Students will become familiar with the shape and appearance of the capital letter 'J'.

Bible Activity

Act out the Bible story. You are Eli. Have the students pretend to be Hannah. Each student should have a stuffed animal to be Samuel.

Have Hannah hold Samuel's hand and walk to see you. Direct Hannah to say, *This is Samuel. He will be your helper.* Then, have Hannah give Samuel to you. Say, *Samuel will live with me and serve God.*

Key Idea: God gave Hannah a son. Hannah remembered her promise to God and took Samuel to live at God's house.

Corresponding Music

The Singing Bible, Disc 2 - Track 7
Song Title: *"Samuel, Samuel"*

Hide and Seek 'J'

Samuel just listens

To what God says.

J-J-Joyfully

He j-j-jumps.

Samuel Listens to God

Fingerplay

Do the fingerplay *"God Sends Samuel"*. Focus on the sound and motion for the letter 'J'.

Key Idea: 'J' = make 2 fingers jump on palm of hand and say *J-J*

Bible Story

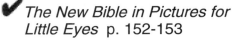

Read the Bible story from **one** of the following resources:

✔ Scripture: 1 Samuel 3:8-10

✔ *A Child's First Bible* p. 82-83

✔ *The New Bible in Pictures for Little Eyes* p. 152-153

Key Idea: God called to Samuel.

Math Activity

Youngers: Have students listen to and repeat simple rhythmic patterns. Examples of patterns include the following: stomp-stomp, stomp-clap, and tap knees-clap.
Olders: Do the activity listed above, but increase the difficulty of the patterns by adding 3 or more motions to each patten. Then, have students create their own patterns for you to repeat as well.

Key Idea: Samuel listened carefully and had to repeat God's words to Eli.

Letter Activity

Copy the *Hide and Seek 'J'* page. Have students circle, color, highlight, or point to the 'J's' on the page. Younger students may need help in order to find any 'J's' at all. It is not necessary to find all the 'J's'. On the bottom of the page, have students connect 'J' to 'j' by tracing the dotted line from left to right.

Key Idea: Students should eventually recognize the capital and small letter 'J' within words.

Bible Activity

Give each student a piece of paper. Help students complete each of the following directions one at a time: Draw two black lines coming down from the top of the page to be God's voice. Draw a yellow, rectangle-shaped pillow on the left side of the page. Draw a blue, square-shaped blanket on the right side of the page. Write the letters 'Y', 'E', 'S' on the bottom of the page.

Key Idea: Samuel heard God's voice as he was sleeping. Samuel answered *Yes* to God.

Corresponding Music

The Singing Bible, Disc 2 - Track 7
Song Title: *"Samuel, Samuel"*

Samuel Listens to God

Fingerplay

Do the fingerplay *"God Sends Samuel"*. Focus on the sound and motion for the letter 'J'.

Key Idea: 'J' = make 2 fingers jump on palm of hand and say *J-J*

Letter Activity

Use the 'J' flashcard from the Appendix. Have students trace the capital and small letter 'J's' on the flashcard with their fingers. Using the flashcard as a model, choose either sidewalk chalk or 2 crayons taped together and paper to write more 'J's'.

Key Idea: Practice the motions needed to make the letter 'J'.

Bible Story

Read the Bible story from **one** of the following resources:

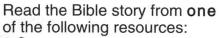 Scripture: 1 Samuel 3:11-13, 4:17-18

 *The New Bible in Pictures for Little Eyes* p. 154-155

Key Idea: Israel turned away from God and lost God's ark.

Bible Activity

Ask students to share some sad things that have happened to them. Possible examples include the following: skinning a knee or an elbow, losing a pet, having a family member die, getting sick, falling down, or losing something special.

Ask, *Is God with you even when sad things happen?* Say, *Praying about it helps us feel better. Let's pray about these sad things now.*

Key Idea: Sad things happened to Israel because they stopped following God. Prayer keeps us close to God.

Dramatic Play

Use a gold colored block to represent God's ark, which was captured by the Philistines. Play *"Capture the Ark"*. Put the "ark" under 1 of 2 cups. Move the cups around and have students guess which cup hides the ark. For older students, use 3 cups instead. Also, allow older students a turn to hide the ark from you.

Key Idea: God let the Philistines capture the ark to show Israel He was no longer with them.

Corresponding Music

None this lesson

Samuel Listens to God

Fingerplay

Do the fingerplay *"God Sends Samuel"*. Focus on the sound and motion for the letter 'J'.

Key Idea: 'J' = make 2 fingers jump on palm of hand and say *J-J*

Bible Story

Read the Bible story from **one** of the following resources:

✔ Scripture: 1 Samuel 9:15-16; 10:1

✔ *A Child's First Bible* p. 84-85

✔ *The New Bible in Pictures for Little Eyes* p. 156-157

Key Idea: Saul becomes king.

Art Activity

Draw a large, oval face on a piece of **white paper** for each student. Have students add the following features to the face using **crayons**: eyes, nose, eyebrows, mouth, and hair. Give each student a **Q-Tip** dipped in **cooking oil** to "paint oil" running down Saul's head from Samuel's annointing.

Key Idea: Saul did not want to be king, but God changed his heart to do what God wanted.

Letter Activity

Use masking tape to make a large 'J' on the floor. Have students place blocks on the tape to trace the letter. Each time a block is placed on the tape, students make the letter **sound**.

Key Idea: Each letter has a name and a sound, just like animals do. For example, a cat may be named Fluffy, but it makes the sound, *Meow.*

Bible Activity

Act out Samuel annointing Saul. You are Samuel, and the students are Saul. Have Saul kneel down. Say, *The Lord God has chosen you to be king of Israel.*

Have Saul bow his head. Pretend to pour oil on Saul's head. Use your fingers to be the oil trickling down Saul's head. Say, *This oil shows everyone you are God's chosen king, and you will answer to God.*

Key Idea: Samuel annointed Saul with oil after God chose Saul to be king.

Corresponding Music

The Singing Bible, Disc 2 - Track 8
Song Title: *"God Gave Them Saul"*

Young David

Fingerplay

Do the fingerplay *"David Will Be King"*. Focus on the sound and motion for the letter 'K'.

Key Idea: 'K' = Clap hands above head toward heaven and say *K-K*

Letter Activity

Copy the 'K' flashcard found in the Appendix. Show the letter side of the flashcard to the students. Read the *Hint* aloud. Demonstrate the motion and sound for 'K'. Have the students repeat it.

Key Idea: Students should eventually do the motion and say the sound for each flashcard without needing a *Hint* or a demonstration.

Bible Story

Read the Bible story from **one** of the following resources:

✔ Scripture: 1 Samuel 17:34-36

✔ *A Child's First Bible* p. 86-89

✔ *The New Bible in Pictures for Little Eyes* p. 158-159

Key Idea: David was a shepherd.

Bible Activity

Act out the Bible story. Have students be David. Set out props to be sheep. Hide some "sheep" away from the flock. Have David walk among the flock watching them. You are a lion coming to attack the sheep. Tell David to swing an imaginary slingshot around in the air to kill the lion. Fall down and pretend to be dead. Have David search for the missing sheep and bring them back. Then, you are a bear attacking the sheep. Tell David to kill the bear with his imaginary slingshot.

Key Idea: As a shepherd, David kept careful watch over his sheep.

Art Activity

Give each student a piece of **green paper**, **6 cotton balls**, and 1/2 a sheet of **white paper**. Have students do the following steps: Tear several clouds out of the white paper and **glue** them near the top of the green paper. Draw and **color** flowers and a river on the green paper.   Glue cotton balls on the green paper in groups of 2 to be sheep. Add 4 stick legs beneath each pair of cotton balls.

Key Idea: David watched over his father's sheep in the fields.

Corresponding Music

The Singing Bible, Disc 2 - Track 10
Song Title: *"Psalm 23"*

Fingerplay: David Will Be King

Days 1-5

David prays and sings.	*Fold hands to pray*
Strum! Strum! Strum!	*Swing hand back and forth*
Praise to God his king	*Point up*
K... K... K...	*Clap hands above head*

David kills a lion.	*Hands around face like a mane*
Roar! Roar! Roar!	*Cup hands around mouth*
David kills Goliath.	*Reach arms up high*
Zip! Zip! Soar!	*Sling motion, round and round*

Does David kill Saul?	*Hold hands like crown on head*
No, No, No!	*Shake head, "No"*
Because our God	*Point up*
Didn't tell him so!	*Shake finger*

Young David

Fingerplay

Do the fingerplay *"David Will Be King"*. Focus on the sound and motion for the letter 'K'.

<u>Key Idea</u>: 'K' = Clap hands above head toward heaven and say *K-K*

Bible Story

Read the Bible story from **one** of the following resources:

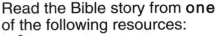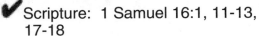

✔ Scripture: 1 Samuel 16:1, 11-13, 17-18

✔ *A Child's First Bible* p. 96-97 (plus the Scripture listed above)

✔ *The New Bible in Pictures for Little Eyes* p. 160-161

<u>Key Idea</u>: David loved God.

Dramatic Play

Use a toy lamb, cotton ball, or other object to be a sheep. Students need a partner to be seated across from them. Either say the words of Psalm 23 or play *"Psalm 23"* from *The Singing Bible* as partners pass the "sheep" back and forth between them. Stop the words or music and see who has the sheep. That person must pat the sheep and say, *The Lord is always with you.*

<u>Key Idea</u>: David wrote Psalm 23. He knew God was always with him.

Letter Activity

Copy the *Hide and Seek 'K'* page. Have students circle, color, highlight, or point to the 'K's' on the page. Younger students may need help in order to find any 'K's' at all. It is not necessary to find all the 'K's'. On the bottom of the page, have students connect 'K' to 'k' by tracing the dotted line from left to right.

<u>Key Idea</u>: Students should eventually recognize the capital and small letter 'K' within words.

Bible Activity

Copy *Count on Me* (in Appendix). Direct students to draw music notes by making black circles that each have a stem in the boxes. Younger students make 2 notes in each box. Older students make 3 notes in each box. Point to each note as you count it with the students. Write the numbers on the lines below each box as you count. Say the numbers below the boxes to count by 2's or by 3's (counting either '2', '4', '6'... or '3', '6', '9' ...).

<u>Key Idea</u>: David enjoyed playing music and singing praises to God.

Corresponding Music

The Singing Bible, Disc 2 – Track 10
Song Title: *"Psalm 23"*

Hide and Seek 'K'

King David prays and sings.

Strum! Strum! Strum!

Praise to God his king.

K... K... K...

K _____ k

K _____ k

Young David

Fingerplay

Do the fingerplay *"David Will Be King"*. Focus on the sound and motion for the letter 'K'.

<u>Key Idea</u>: 'K' = Clap hands above head toward heaven and say *K-K*

Bible Story

Read the Bible story from **one** of the following resources:

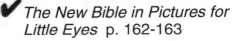

✔ Scripture: 1 Samuel 17:45-49

✔ *A Child's First Bible* p. 90-91

✔ *The New Bible in Pictures for Little Eyes* p. 162-163

<u>Key Idea</u>: David killed Goliath.

Math Activity

<u>Youngers</u>: Choose 3 stuffed animals or other toys for students to put in order from smallest to biggest. Add more toys to increase the difficulty of the activity. <u>Olders</u>: Set out 1 small object. Have students find an object that is bigger than the first object and set it beside the first one. Repeat this process until the objects get too big. Then, name 2 objects and have students say which one is bigger.

<u>Key Idea</u>: Goliath was bigger, but God helped David win anyway.

Letter Activity

Use masking tape to make a large 'K' on the floor. Have students drive a toy car or other toy vehicle on the tape to trace the letter. Have students say the letter **sound** as they drive.

<u>Key Idea</u>: Each letter has a name and a sound, just like animals do. For example, a dog may be named Rover, but it makes the sound, *Ruff.*

Bible Activity

Give each student a piece of paper. Help students complete each of the following directions one at a time: Draw a brown hook on the left side of the page to be a shepherd's staff. Draw five gray circles on the right side of the page to be stones. Draw a line from the stones to the bottom of the page. Tell students, *We drew a line to show that David hit Goliath with a stone, and Goliath fell down dead.*

<u>Key Idea</u>: God helped David, the shepherd boy, beat Goliath with a sling and a stone.

Corresponding Music

The Singing Bible, Disc 2 – Track 9
Song Title: *"David"*

Young David

Fingerplay

Do the fingerplay *"David Will Be King."* Focus on the sound and motion for the letter 'K'.

<u>Key Idea</u>: 'K' = Clap hands above head toward heaven and say *K-K*

Bible Story

Read the Bible story from **one** of the following resources:

✔ Scripture: 1 Samuel 20:31-33, 42

✔ *A Child's First Bible* p. 92-93

✔ *The New Bible in Pictures for Little Eyes* p. 164-165

<u>Key Idea</u>: Jonathan and David

Active Exploration

<u>Youngers</u>: Whisper a word or a sentence in a student's ear. That student whispers the same thing to the next student or back to you. Ideas to whisper include the following: *friend, happy, love, I like you. I am happy. I like to talk to you.*
<u>Olders</u>: Do the same activity above, except whisper about the story instead. Ideas to whisper include the following: *Jonathan is kind. David will be king. David and Jonathan are friends.*

<u>Key Idea</u>: David trusted Jonathan.

Letter Activity

Write a big 'K' on a piece of paper. Have students glue cotton balls or pieces of yarn to the letter. Younger students will need you to apply drops of glue on the letter for them first.

<u>Key Idea</u>: Students will become familiar with the shape and appearance of the capital letter 'K'.

Bible Activity

Say, *David and Jonathan were good friends. Let's use our stuffed animals to practice being good friends.*

Have students act out some of the following examples with their stuffed animals: sharing toys or food, taking turns, saying nice things, forgiving each other, asking each other's opinion, asking to use their things before taking them, and giving the best of what they have to their friend.

<u>Key Idea</u>: David and Jonathan were good friends. Jonathan saved David's life because he was David's friend.

Corresponding Music

The Singing Bible, Disc 2 – Track 9
Song Title: *"David"*

Young David

Fingerplay

Do the fingerplay *"David Will Be King"*. Focus on the sound and motion for the letter 'K'.

<u>Key Idea:</u> 'K' = Clap hands above head toward heaven and say *K-K*

Bible Story

Read the Bible story from **one** of the following resources:

✔ Scripture: 1 Samuel 26:7-12

✔ *A Child's First Bible* p. 94-95

✔ *The New Bible in Pictures for Little Eyes* p. 166-167

<u>Key Idea:</u> David saved Saul.

Devotional Activity

Read and discuss the devotion from **one** of the following resources:

✔ *Big Thoughts for Little People*
Read the two pages for letter 'K'.

✔ *Teach Them to Your Children*
Read the two pages for letter 'K'.

✔ *My ABC Bible Verses*
Read the two pages for letter 'K'.

<u>Key Idea:</u> Share a devotional focusing on character traits or memory work based on the letter 'K'.

Letter Activity

Use the 'K' flashcard from the Appendix. Have students trace the capital and small letter 'K' on the flashcard with their fingers. Using the flashcard as a model, give students either a small amount of cooking oil or liquid soap on an aluminum pan or plate to use to write more 'K's'.

<u>Key Idea:</u> Practice the motions needed to make the letter 'K'.

Bible Activity

Act out the Bible story. Have students be David. Lay a pillow on the floor to be Saul sleeping.

Give the following directions to the students: *Put your finger to your lips and say, "Shhh". Tiptoe over to Saul. Put your hand out to stop your friend from spearing Saul. Shake your head, "No". Bend down and take Saul's spear and jug. Tiptoe away from Saul. Say, "God tells us what to do."*

<u>Key Idea:</u> Saul was trying to kill David, but David did not hurt Saul.

Corresponding Music

None this lesson

King David

Fingerplay

Do the fingerplay *"David Learns to Lead"*. Focus on the sound and motion for the letter 'L'.

<u>Key Idea</u>: 'L' = Swing hand back and forth as if playing a harp and say *L-L*

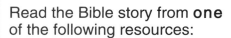

Bible Story

Read the Bible story from **one** of the following resources:

 Scripture: 2 Samuel 2:4-7

 The New Bible in Pictures for Little Eyes p. 168-169

<u>Key Idea</u>: David became king.

Dramatic Play

You are King David. The students must obey you. Set out several stuffed animals or play figures that have names. Give directions of things for the students to do with the figures. Let older students be David and give directions for you to follow using the play figures. Possible directions include the following: Shake Emma's paw. Have Boris bow. Make Duncan jump. Lift Fluffy's hands in the air.

<u>Key Idea</u>: God chose David to be king. The people obeyed him.

Letter Activity

Copy the 'L' flashcard found in the Appendix. Show the letter side of the flashcard to the students. Read the *Hint* aloud. Demonstrate the motion and sound for 'L'. Have the students repeat it.

<u>Key Idea</u>: Students should eventually do the motion and say the sound for each flashcard without needing a *Hint* or a demonstration.

Bible Activity

Copy *Count on Me* (in Appendix). Direct students to draw jewels by making different colored diamonds in the boxes. Younger students make 2 jewels in each box. Older students make 3 jewels in each box. Point to each jewel as you count it with the students. Write the numbers on the lines below each box as you count. Say the numbers below the boxes to count by 2's or by 3's (counting either '2', '4', '6'... or '3', '6', '9' ...).

<u>Key Idea</u>: After Saul died, David asked the Lord if he should move back home. Then, he became King.

Corresponding Music

The Singing Bible, Disc 2 – Track 9
Song Title: *"David"*

Fingerplay: David Learns to Lead
(Sing to the tune of *"Hickory, Dickory, Dock"*)

David learned to lead.	*Make beckoning motion with hand*
His people loved the Lord.	*Cross arms on chest; Point up*
God's ark came home.	*Fold hands*
Sing to the Lord.	*Cup hands around mouth*
L... L... L... L... L...	*Swing hand back and forth*

David learned a lesson.	*Point to mind*
To listen to the Lord.	*Cup hand around ear; Point up*
His sin was forgiven.	*Hug arms around self*
Sing praises to heaven.	*Cup hands around mouth*
L... L... L... L... L...	*Swing hand back and forth*

King David

Fingerplay

Do the fingerplay *"David Learns to Lead"*. Focus on the sound and motion for the letter 'L'.

Key Idea: 'L' = Swing hand back and forth as if playing a harp and say *L-L*

Bible Story

Read the Bible story from **one** of the following resources:

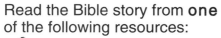 Scripture: 2 Samuel 6:12-15

 *A Child's First Bible* p. 98-99

 *The New Bible in Pictures for Little Eyes* p. 170-171

Key Idea: God's ark came home.

Art Activity

Students need a **small empty box** to use for God's ark. Ideas for boxes include the following: a jello or pudding box, macaroni and cheese box, bar soap box, toothpaste box, or rice box. Provide items for students to glue on the ark in a collage. Possible items include the following: foil, dry cereal, wrapping paper, macaroni noodles, raisins, marshmallows, material, and ribbon.

Key Idea: God's ark held the laws and was very special and beautiful.

Letter Activity

Use masking tape to make a large 'L' on the floor. Have students tiptoe on the tape to trace the letter. Then, have students jump off the end of the letter saying the letter **sound** as they jump.

Key Idea: Each letter has a name and a sound, just like animals do. For example, a horse may be named Silver, but it makes the sound, *Neigh.*

Bible Activity

Have students make a procession to celebrate God's ark. Use the ark from today's *Art Activity* or another prop to be the ark. You carry the ark and tell the students to follow behind singing praise songs to God.

Possible praise songs include the following: *"God Is So Good"*, *"Rise and Shine"*, *"Heavenly Sunshine"*, *"Praise Ye the Lord"*, and *"If You're Happy and You Know It"*.

Key Idea: David and the people celebrated God's ark coming home.

Corresponding Music

The Singing Bible, Disc 2 – Track 11
Song Title: *"Psalm 150"*

King David

Fingerplay

Do the fingerplay *"David Learns to Lead"*. Focus on the sound and motion for the letter 'L'.

Key Idea: 'L' = Swing hand back and forth as if playing a harp and say *L-L*

Bible Story

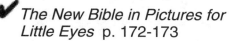

Read the Bible story from **one** of the following resources:

✔ Scripture: 2 Samuel 12:7-10

✔ *A Child's First Bible* p. 100-101

✔ *The New Bible in Pictures for Little Eyes* p. 172-173

Key Idea: David sinned.

Active Exploration

Tell students, *If I say a good thing, jump up and shout, "Yeah, that's good!" If I say a bad thing, kneel face down and say, "No, no, that's bad!"* Possible ideas of good and bad things to list include the following: sharing, sneaking candy before dinner, thanking God, running into the street, hitting your brother, praying, grabbing a toy from someone, giving a hug, and smiling.

Key Idea: David did a bad thing, and God punished him for it.

Letter Activity

Copy the *Hide and Seek 'L'* page. Have students circle, color, highlight, or point to the 'L's' on the page. Younger students may need help in order to find any 'L's' at all. It is not necessary to find all the 'L's'. On the bottom of the page, have students connect 'L' to 'l' by tracing the dotted line from left to right.

Key Idea: Students should eventually recognize the capital and small letter 'L' within words.

Bible Activity

Give each student a piece of paper. Help students complete each of the following directions one at a time: Draw a yellow oval on the left side of the page to be a crown. Write the letters 'N', 'O' on the right side of the page. Draw a circle with a frown in it at the bottom of the page to show King David's face. Draw a line from the word, *No,* to the face at the bottom of the page.

Key Idea: Nathan told King David that he had done something wrong. David was sorry.

Corresponding Music

None this lesson

Hide and Seek 'L'

David learned to lead.

His people loved the Lord.

God's ark came home.

Sing to the Lord.

L... L... L... L... L...

L _____ l

L _____ l

King David

Fingerplay

Do the fingerplay *"David Learns to Lead"*. Focus on the sound and motion for the letter 'L'.

<u>Key Idea</u>: 'L' = Swing hand back and forth as if playing a harp and say *L-L*

Bible Story

Reread the Bible story from day 3 in **one** of the following resources:

✔ Scripture: 2 Samuel 12:7-10
✔ *A Child's First Bible* p. 100-101
✔ *The New Bible in Pictures for Little Eyes* p. 172-173

<u>Key Idea</u>: God forgave David.

Devotional Activity

Read and discuss the devotion from **one** of the following resources:

✔ *Big Thoughts for Little People*
Read the two pages for letter 'L'.

✔ *Teach Them to Your Children*
Read the two pages for letter 'L'.

✔ *My ABC Bible Verses*
Read the two pages for letter 'L'.

<u>Key Idea</u>: Share a devotional focusing on character traits or memory work based on the letter 'L'.

Letter Activity

Write a big 'L' on a piece of paper. Have students glue dried macaroni or raisins to the letter. Younger students will need you to apply drops of glue on the letter for them first.

<u>Key Idea</u>: Students will become familiar with the shape and appearance of the capital letter 'L'.

Bible Activity

Explain to students that husbands should watch over their wives, and brothers should watch over their sisters. Some polite ways for men to show respect to women include the following: opening the door for them, holding their coat open for them, waiting to go second, introducing the woman first, waiting for a woman to be seated before the man sits, and pushing in the woman's chair for her.

Have students practice these behaviors using a stuffed animal for a woman.

<u>Key Idea</u>: David did not follow God's laws when he married Bathsheba.

Corresponding Music

None this lesson

King David

Fingerplay

Do the fingerplay *"David Learns to Lead"*. Focus on the sound and motion for the letter 'L'.

Key Idea: 'L' = Swing hand back and forth as if playing a harp and say *L-L*

Bible Story

Read the Bible story from **one** of the following resources:

✔ Scripture: 2 Samuel 18:9-10, 15, 33

✔ *A Child's First Bible* p. 102-103

✔ *The New Bible in Pictures for Little Eyes* p. 174-175

Key Idea: Absalom was not king.

Math Activity

Give each student a 12" piece of yarn or string (to be Absalom's long hair) and a white piece of paper with a tree branch drawn at the top. Have students cut their yarn into pieces, find the piece that is the longest, and glue it hanging from the tree branch. Continue ordering and gluing the rest of the pieces from longest to shortest on the branch.

Key Idea: Absalom was caught.

Letter Activity

Use the 'L' flashcard from the Appendix. Have students trace the capital and small letter 'L' on the flashcard with their fingers. Using the flashcard as a model, choose either pudding, chocolate syrup, baby food, or fingerpaint on a plate, pan, or piece of paper for students to write more 'L's'.

Key Idea: Practice the motions needed to make the letter 'L'.

Bible Activity

Have students use props to act out the story of Absalom and his death. Show Absalom riding on his mule. As the mule passes under a tree, Absalom's hair gets caught in the branches. Since the mule keeps on walking, Absalom is left hanging. Joab comes and spears Absalom. Say, *Absalom was evil. God didn't want him to be king.*

Key Idea: Absalom fought against his own father, David, to be king. God did not let Absalom win.

Corresponding Music

None this lesson

King Solomon

Fingerplay

Do the fingerplay *"What Do You Know?"* Focus on reviewing the sounds and motions for the letters.

Key Idea: Practice the sounds and motions for the letters 'A-L'.

Bible Story

Read the Bible story from **one** of the following resources:

✔ Scripture: 1 Kings 3:23-28; 4:29
✔ *A Child's First Bible* p. 104-107
✔ *The New Bible in Pictures for Little Eyes* p. 176-177

Key Idea: God made Solomon wise.

Math Activity

Put 5 or more different sized pairs of shoes or socks into a pile. Have students find matching pairs and put them in order from smallest to largest. Have students try on the pairs and walk around. Describe each pair as too large, too small, or just right for the students' feet. Older students may also be asked to sort pairs by color or design.

Key Idea: Solomon was wise and knew how to match the birth mother with her baby. Can you be wise and make some matches too?

Letter Activity

This is a review week. Review all the flashcards from the previous weeks. Show the letter side of each flashcard to the students. Have them respond with the motion and sound. If needed, read the *Hint* or demonstrate the motion and sound.

Key Idea: Students should eventually do the motion and say the sound for each flashcard without needing a *Hint* or a demonstration from you.

Bible Activity

Give each student a piece of paper. Help students complete each of the following directions one at a time:

Draw a blue cloud at the top of the page to show Solomon's dream. Draw a red smile in the middle of the page. Draw a yellow rectangle at the bottom of the page to show the temple.

Key Idea: God came to Solomon in a dream. Solomon asked to be wise. God made Solomon wise. Solomon built God's temple.

Corresponding Music

The Singing Bible, Disc 3 – Tracks 1, 2
Song Titles: *"Solomon"*
                 "Listen to Wisdom"

Fingerplay: What Do You Know?

Days 1-5

We've learned about *A-A-Adam*	*Hands on cheeks in surprise*
And *B-B-Boat,*	*Hug yourself and rock side-to-side*
C-C-Clippity clop	*Tap palms on thighs in rhythm*
And *D-D-Dusty* camel.	*Hold reins, move up and down*
E-E-Empty jars	*Shake hand to shake empty jar*
And *F-F-Fire,*	*Wiggle 10 fingers like flames*
G-G-Gurgle	*Hold nose, put hand up*
And *H-H-Helping* hands.	*Lace fingers, move up and down*
I-Impossible	*Push palms up as if lifting*
And *J-J-Joyful* jumping,	*2 fingers jump on palm of hand*
K-K-clapping hands	*Clap hands above head*
And *L-L-La-La-La.*	*Swing hand back and forth*
Now, as Solomon	*Bow head*
Asks for wisdom,	*Fold hands to pray*
God has Solomon	*Point up*
Build the temple.	*Tap fists on top of one another*
Just like the others	*Open palms together like Bible*
God has plans for you too.	*Point up, then point to yourself*
Never forget	*Shake head, "No"*
What God can do!	*Spread arms wide*

King Solomon

Fingerplay

Do the fingerplay *"What Do You Know?"* Focus on reviewing the sounds and motions for the letters.

<u>Key Idea</u>: Practice the sounds and motions for the letters 'A-L'.

Bible Story

Read the Bible story from **one** of the following resources:

✔ Scripture: 1 Kings 5:3-5; 6:11-13

✔ *A Child's First Bible* p. 108-109

✔ *The New Bible in Pictures for Little Eyes* p. 178-179

<u>Key Idea</u>: Solomon built the temple.

Art Activity

Give students **marshmallows** and **toothpicks** or **uncooked spaghetti** to build a "Temple" or a "House for God". Students may break the spaghetti or toothpicks as needed to form their sculptures. Younger students may use larger marshmallows to make the sculpting easier.

<u>Key Idea</u>: Solomon built a temple for the Lord, just as God had said David's son would do when he was king.

Letter Activity

Choose one or more of the letters 'A-L' to review. Use masking tape to make the large review letter on the floor. Have students sit on a pillow and scoot on the tape to trace the letter. Have students say the letter **sound** as they scoot.

<u>Key Idea</u>: Each letter has a name and a sound, just like animals do. For example, a cow may be named Bessie, but it makes the sound, *Moo.*

Bible Activity

Have students act out the following building motions as you say them: *swing axes to cut down trees, saw wood, pound nails, stir gold in a pot over a fire, press gold onto walls, stomp clay with feet, mix clay with hands, lift heavy bricks on top of each other, and sew cloth with thread.*

<u>Key Idea</u>: To show honor to God as the temple was built, no hammering or pounding was done at the temple. Instead, it was done far away.

Corresponding Music

The Singing Bible, Disc 3 – Track 1, 3
Song Titles: *"Solomon"*
"The Temple"

King Solomon

Fingerplay

Do the fingerplay *"What Do You Know?"* Focus on reviewing the sounds and motions for the letters.

<u>Key Idea</u>: Practice the sounds and motions for the letters 'A-L'.

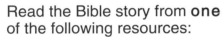

Bible Story

Read the Bible story from **one** of the following resources:

 Scripture: 1 Kings 9:1-7

 The New Bible in Pictures for Little Eyes p. 180-181

<u>Key Idea</u>: The people gave thanks for the temple.

Dramatic Play

Each student needs a "musical instrument". These may be real instruments or pots and spoons for drums, two kettle lids for cymbals, two spoons for rhythm sticks, or oatmeal containers for shakers. Students march around playing the instruments. Every once and awhile signal the students to stop and take turns finishing the sentence, *Thank you God for _____.*

<u>Key Idea</u>: Israel celebrated when God's temple was finished.

Letter Activity

Choose one letter from 'A-L' to review. Write that letter on a big piece of paper. Use water to thin glue and have students "paint" the glue on the letter. Then, sprinkle either salt, coffee grounds, glitter, or any kind of spice on the glue. Younger students will need you to help them with the sprinkling part.

<u>Key Idea</u>: Students will become familiar with the shape and appearance of the capital letters.

Bible Activity

Have students share things they are thankful to have. Possible examples include the following: family, food, church, home, clothes, toys, friends, and the Bible. Say, *Let's praise God for the many blessings He has given us. Raise your hands toward heaven while we pray a prayer of thanks.* Say a prayer and include the things the students mentioned.

<u>Key Idea</u>: Solomon and the people praised God for blessing them. They promised to follow God.

Corresponding Music

The Singing Bible, Disc 3 – Track 1, 3
Song Titles: *"Solomon"*
          "The Temple"

King Solomon

Fingerplay

Do the fingerplay *"What Do You Know?"* Focus on reviewing the sounds and motions for the letters.

Key Idea: Practice the sounds and motions for the letters 'A-L'.

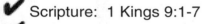

Bible Story

Reread the Bible story from day 2 in **one** of the following resources:

✔ Scripture: 1 Kings 9:1-7

✔ *The New Bible in Pictures for Little Eyes* p. 180-181

Key Idea: The people gave thanks for the temple.

Devotional Activity

Read and discuss the devotion from **one** of the following resources:

✔ *Big Thoughts for Little People*
Review verses for 'I', 'J', 'K', 'L'

✔ *Teach Them to Your Children*
Review verses for 'I', 'J', 'K', 'L'

✔ *My ABC Bible Verses*
Review verses for 'I', 'J', 'K', 'L'

Key Idea: Share a devotional focusing on character traits or memory work based on the letters 'I', 'J', 'K', 'L'.

Letter Activity

Copy the *Hide-n-Seek Review* page. Choose a letter from 'I-L' to review. Have students circle, color, highlight, or point to the chosen letter. Younger students may need help in order to find any of the chosen letters. On the bottom of the page, have students draw a line to connect each capital letter to its matching small letter.

Key Idea: Students should eventually recognize the capital and small letters 'I-L' within words.

Bible Activity

Copy *Count on Me* (in Appendix). Direct students to draw crosses by making brown 't's' in each of the boxes. Younger students make 2 crosses in each box. Older students make 3 crosses in each box. Point to each cross as you count it with the students. Write the numbers on the lines below each box as you count. Say the numbers below the boxes to count by 2's or by 3's (counting either '2', '4', '6'... or '3', '6', '9' ...).

Key Idea: We need to go to church.

Corresponding Music

The Singing Bible, Disc 3 – Track 1, 3
Song Titles: *"Solomon"*
             "The Temple"

Hide and Seek Review

We've learned about I-Impossible,

And J-J-Joyful jumping,

K-K-King David,

And La-La-La-La-La.

I
J
K
L

j
k
i
l

King Solomon

Unit 15 - Day 5

Fingerplay

Do the fingerplay *"What Do You Know?"* Focus on reviewing the sounds and motions for the letters.

Key Idea: Practice the sounds and motions for the letters 'A-L'.

Bible Story

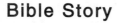

Read the Bible story from **one** of the following resources:

✔ Scripture: 1 Kings 11:1-2, 9-12

✔ *A Child's First Bible* p. 110-111

✔ *The New Bible in Pictures for Little Eyes* p. 182-183

Key Idea: Solomon worshipped an idol.

Active Exploration

Model pairs of actions that are opposites for the students to repeat. Possible actions include the following: step left and right, jump forward and backward, reach high and low, stand up and sit down, twirl fast and slow, raise hands up and down, show eyes open and closed, clap loudly and softly, swing arms out and in, and tiptoe quickly and slowly.

Key Idea: Worshiping an idol was the opposite of what God said to do.

Letter Activity

Choose one or more of the flashcards from the previous weeks to review. Have students trace the capital and small letters on the flashcards with their fingers. Using the flashcards as models, choose either markers and markerboards or pieces of carpet and fingers to practice writing more letters.

Key Idea: Practice the motions needed to make the letters.

Bible Activity

Act out the Bible story. Use props for Solomon, some of his wives, and an idol. Have the "wives" say, *Pray to our gods. They are stronger than your God.* Tell the students to shout, *No! No! Don't do it Solomon!*

Make Solomon bow down to the idol. Tell the students to shout their previous warning again.   Make Solomon pray to the idol. Tell the students to warn him again.

Key Idea: Solomon listened to his wives, and they turned him away from God.

Corresponding Music

The Singing Bible, Disc 3 – Track 1, 2
Song Titles: *"Solomon"*
              "Listen to Wisdom"

Elijah and Elisha

Fingerplay

Do the fingerplay *"Miracles"*. Focus on the sound and motion for the letter 'M'.

Key Idea: 'M' = put hand over mouth, pull it away, and say *M-M*

Letter Activity

Copy the 'M' flashcard found in the Appendix. Show the letter side of the flashcard to the students. Read the *Hint* aloud. Demonstrate the motion and sound for 'M'. Have the students repeat it.

Key Idea: Students should eventually do the motion and say the sound for each flashcard without needing a *Hint* or a demonstration.

Bible Story

Read the Bible story from **one** of the following resources:

 Scripture: 1 Kings 16:30; 17:1-4

 A Child's First Bible p. 112-113

✔ *The New Bible in Pictures for Little Eyes* p. 184-185

Key Idea: Ravens fed Elijah.

Bible Activity

Copy *Count on Me* (in Appendix). Direct students to draw birds by making black squiggles in each of the boxes. Younger students make 2 birds in each box. Older students make 3 birds in each box. Point to each bird as you count it with the students. Write the numbers on the lines below each box as you count. Say the numbers below the boxes to count by 2's or by 3's (counting either '2', '4', '6'... or '3', '6', '9' ...).

Key Idea: There was no rain because God was punishing King Ahab. But, God made sure his prophet, Elijah, had food and water.

Math Activity

Mix 3 or more kinds of "dry" finger foods together. Possible finger foods include crackers, cereals, baking chips, pretzels, marshmallows, raisins, or chips.

Have students pretend to be birds bringing food to Elijah, picking up one piece of food at a time and sorting it into a muffin tin or other container.

Key Idea: God commanded the ravens to bring food to Elijah.

Corresponding Music

The Singing Bible, Disc 3 – Track 4
Song Title: *"Elijah"*

Fingerplay: Miracles
(Sing to the tune of *"Frere Jacques"*)

Birds fed Elijah.	*Flap arms like wings*
He made a boy alive.	*Tap heart with hand*
M-Miracles	*Pat hand over mouth, pull it away*
M-Miracles	*Pat hand over mouth, pull it away*
Fire came from heaven.	*Wiggle 10 fingers like flames*
A chariot he left in.	*Hold reins; moving up and down*
M-Miracles	*Pat hand over mouth, pull it away*
M-Miracles	*Pat hand over mouth, pull it away*

Elijah was gone.	*Point up to the sky*
Elisha carried on.	*Salute*
M-Miracles	*Pat hand over mouth, pull it away*
M-Miracles	*Pat hand over mouth, pull it away*
A man's skin was healed.	*Rub arms with hands*
A holy army was near.	*Marching motions with arms*
M-Miracles	*Pat hand over mouth, pull it away*
M-Miracles	*Pat hand over mouth, pull it away*

Elijah and Elisha

Fingerplay

Do the fingerplay *"Miracles"*. Focus on the sound and motion for the letter 'M'.

<u>Key Idea</u>: 'M' = put hand over mouth, pull it away, and say *M-M*

Bible Story

Read the Bible story from **one** of the following resources:

Scripture: 1 Kings 18:21-24, 38; 2 Kings 2:1, 11-14

A Child's First Bible p. 114-117 (plus the Scripture listed above)

The New Bible in Pictures for Little Eyes p. 188-191

<u>Key Idea</u>: God sent fire to the altar and to take Elijah to heaven.

Art Activity

Each student needs **playdough** to make a model of Elijah's altar. Show students how to roll the dough to make a pile of round rocks. Have students roll dough to make sticks to put on top of the rock pile. Press dough around the base of the pile to look like water. Tell students to make playdough flames to put on top of the rocks and sticks.

<u>Key Idea</u>: God sent fire from the sky in answer to Elijah's prayer.

Letter Activity

Use masking tape to make a large 'M' on the floor. Have students walk a stuffed animal on the tape to trace the letter. Then, have students walk the letter themselves, saying the letter **sound** as they walk.

<u>Key Idea</u>: Each letter has a name and a sound, just like animals do. For example, a pig may be named Pinky, but it makes the sound, *Oink.*

Bible Activity

Act out Elijah being taken to heaven. The students are Elisha. You are Elijah. Tell the students to walk along the road and stop at the river. Now, you take off your coat and hit the water to make it part. Walk across. Say, *Cover your ears as you hear wind. Shield your eyes, point, and look up in the sky. God has taken Elijah to heaven. Lean down, pick up Elijah's coat, and hit the water. Cross the river on dry ground.* Say, "The God of Elijah is with me too."

<u>Key Idea</u>: After Elijah was taken to heaven, Elisha was God's prophet.

Corresponding Music

The Singing Bible, Disc 3 – Track 4
Song Title: *"Elijah"*

Elijah and Elisha

Fingerplay

Do the fingerplay *"Miracles"*. Focus on the sound and motion for the letter 'M'.

<u>Key Idea</u>: 'M' = put hand over mouth, pull it away, and say *M-M*

Letter Activity

Write a big 'M' on a piece of paper. Have students glue dry 'O'-shaped cereal or dried beans to the letter. Younger students will need you to apply drops of glue on the letter for them first.

<u>Key Idea</u>: Students will become familiar with the shape and appearance of the capital letter 'M'.

Bible Story

Read the Bible story from **one** of the following resources:

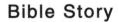 Scripture: 2 Kings 4:1-7

A Child's First Bible p. 118-119

The New Bible in Pictures for Little Eyes p. 192-193

<u>Key Idea</u>: The oil kept flowing.

Bible Activity

Act out the story of the oil that didn't run out. Place bowls at different spots around the room to represent empty "jars". Each of these spots will be a neighbor's "house". Have students pretend to knock on the door of each house and collect the jars inside. Designate a central place for students to put the jars they collect. Tell students to pretend to fill the empty jars with oil one at a time. Lead students in kneeling and thanking God for taking care of them.

<u>Key Idea</u>: Elisha asked God to help the lady save her boys by giving her plenty of oil to sell to pay her debts.

Dramatic Play

Measure 1 cup of water. Add yellow food coloring to the water, so it looks like oil. Let students pour a small amount of "oil" into other containers until the cup is empty. Older students may measure and pour the oil by 1/2 or 1/4 cups until it is gone. Say, *The oil in your cup is gone. God made the oil in the story keep flowing until every jar was filled. Can you do that?*

<u>Key Idea</u>: God kept the oil flowing until the lady had all she needed.

Corresponding Music

None this lesson

Elijah and Elisha

Fingerplay

Do the fingerplay *"Miracles"*. Focus on the sound and motion for the letter 'M'.

Key Idea: 'M' = put hand over mouth, pull it away, and say *M-M*

Bible Story

Read the Bible story from **one** of the following resources:

✔ Scripture: 2 Kings 5:1-3, 9-10, 14-15

✔ *A Child's First Bible* p. 122-123

✔ *The New Bible in Pictures for Little Eyes* p. 194-197

Key Idea: Naaman was healed.

Active Exploration

Pour 1 cup of powdered laundry detergent and 1/8 cup of water into a small ziplock bag for each student. Zip each bag closed. Have students squeeze the bag to mix the contents. Unzip each bag and turn it inside out, scraping the contents onto waxed paper. Tell students to mold the mixture into a bar of soap. Let it dry and use it as hand soap.

Key Idea: God healed Naaman when Naaman washed in the river.

Letter Activity

Copy the *Hide and Seek 'M'* page. Have students circle, color, highlight, or point to the 'M's' on the page. Younger students may need help in order to find any 'M's' at all. It is not necessary to find all the 'M's'. On the bottom of the page, have students connect 'M' to 'm' by tracing the dotted line from left to right.

Key Idea: Students should eventually recognize the capital and small letter 'M' within words.

Bible Activity

Give each student a piece of paper. Help students complete each of the following directions one at a time: Draw red circles at the top of the page to be sores. Draw a blue, wavy line in the middle of the page to be a river. Draw a red smile at the bottom of the page.

Key Idea: Naaman had sores on his body. Elisha told Naaman to wash in the river, and God would heal him. Naaman was healed.

Corresponding Music

None this lesson

Hide and Seek 'M'

A man's skin was healed.

A holy army was near.

M-Miracles!

M-Miracles!

Elijah and Elisha

Fingerplay

Do the fingerplay *"Miracles"*. Focus on the sound and motion for the letter 'M'.

Key Idea: 'M' = put hand over mouth, pull it away, and say *M-M*

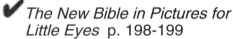

Bible Story

Read the Bible story from **one** of the following resources:

✔ Scripture: 2 Kings 6:8-10, 15-17

✔ *The New Bible in Pictures for Little Eyes* p. 198-199

Key Idea: God sent his angels to help Elisha.

Devotional Activity

Read and discuss the devotion from **one** of the following resources:

✔ *Big Thoughts for Little People*
Read the two pages for letter 'M'.

✔ *Teach Them to Your Children*
Read the two pages for letter 'M'.

✔ *My ABC Bible Verses*
Read the two pages for letter 'M'.

Key Idea: Share a devotional focusing on character traits or memory work based on the letter 'M'.

Letter Activity

Use the 'M' flashcard from the Appendix. Have students trace the capital and small letter 'M's' on the flashcard with their fingers. Using the flashcard as a model, choose either a bar of soap on a mirror or an ice cube on construction paper to write more 'M's'.

Key Idea: Practice the motions needed to make the letter 'M'.

Bible Activity

Read some of the following Scriptures about angels from the Bible: Psalms 103:20-21, Hebrews 1:14, Psalms 91:11-12, and Revelation 19:9-10. Emphasize that God created the angels. We should never pray to or worship an angel. God's angels must obey him and do his will. Pray with the students and thank God for his angels.

Key Idea: God's angels are his helpers. He sends them to watch over us and to help us.

Corresponding Music

None this lesson

The Time of the Kings

Fingerplay

Do the fingerplay *"This Little King"*. Focus on the sound and motion for the letter 'N'.

<u>Key Idea</u>: 'N' = tap top of hand twice with 2 fingers of other hand and say *N-N*

Bible Story

Read the Bible story from **one** of the following resources:

✔ Scripture: 2 Chronicles 24:1-4, 13, 17-18

✔ *A Child's First Bible* p. 124-125

✔ *The New Bible in Pictures for Little Eyes* p. 200-201

<u>Key Idea</u>: Joash fixed the temple.

Active Exploration

On **heavy white paper** use a **permanent marker** to draw a simple wall with many cracks in it. This wall is God's house that needs fixing. Mix **cornmeal** or **dry oats** with **warm water** to make a thick paste. Have students press the paste on each crack to "patch" the wall. Discuss the texture of the paste.

<u>Key Idea</u>: Joash made sure God's house was repaired.

Letter Activity

Copy the 'N' flashcard found in the Appendix. Show the letter side of the flashcard to the students. Read the *Hint* aloud. Demonstrate the motion and sound for 'N'. Have the students repeat it.

<u>Key Idea</u>: Students should eventually do the motion and say the sound for each flashcard without needing a *Hint* or a demonstration.

Bible Activity

Copy *Count on Me* (in Appendix). Direct students to draw pillars by making gold rectangles in each of the boxes. Younger students make 2 pillars in each box. Older students make 3 pillars in each box. Point to each pillar as you count it. Write the numbers on the lines below each box as you count. Say the numbers below the boxes to count by 2's or by 3's (counting either '2', '4', '6'... or '3', '6', '9' ...).

<u>Key Idea</u>: Young King Joash listened to God's prophet, Jehoiada, and fixed God's temple.

Corresponding Music

The Singing Bible, Disc 3 – Track 5
Song Title: *"Oh, Israel Turn Back to God"*

Fingerplay: This Little King

Days 1-5

This little king Makes God's house new.	*Wiggle pinky toe or finger*
This next king Gets some bad news.	*Wiggle fourth toe or finger*
This good king Is reading God's book.	*Wiggle third toe or finger*
This bad king Is *N-N-Naughty* next.	*Wiggle second toe or finger* *Tap top of hand with 2 fingers*
This nice king, Lets the Israelites go...	*Wiggle big toe or thumb*
Walking, walking, walking All the way back home.	*Walk fingers quickly up leg or arm* *Tickle under arm*

Hide and Seek 'N'

This next king

Is reading God's book.

This bad king

Is N-N-Naughty next.

The Time of the Kings

Fingerplay

Do the fingerplay *"This Little King"*. Focus on the sound and motion for the letter 'N'.

Key Idea: 'N' = tap top of hand twice with 2 fingers of other hand and say *N-N*

Bible Story

Read the Bible story from **one** of the following resources:

✔ Scripture: 2 Kings 18:3-7

✔ *A Child's First Bible* p. 128-129

✔ *The New Bible in Pictures for Little Eyes* p. 202-203

Key Idea: Hezekiah served God.

Art Activity

Cut a **long strip of paper** about 1" wide for each student. The strip should be long enough to fit around each student's head like a crown. Provide a **variety of items** for students to use **to decorate** their crowns. Possible decorative items include glitter, colored cereal, yarn, thin strips of aluminum foil, special markers, and colored paper. Tape the strips into crowns after they dry.

Key Idea: King Hezekiah listened to Isaiah and followed God closely.

Letter Activity

Copy the *Hide and Seek 'N'* page. Have students circle, color, highlight, or point to the 'N's on the page. Younger students may need help in order to find any 'N's at all. It is not necessary to find all the 'N's. On the bottom of the page, have students connect 'N' to 'n' by tracing the dotted line from left to right.

Key Idea: Students should eventually recognize the capital and small letter 'N' within words.

Bible Activity

Have students wear the crowns from the *Art Activity* and pretend to be King Hezekiah. Have them perform the following actions: swing a hammer to smash idols, sing a praise song such as *"God Is So Good"*, open a "letter" and look scared, run to the temple, kneel down, ask God to save Judah from Assyria, thank God for saving you, lay down and act sick, ask God for help, praise God for healing you.

Key Idea: King Hezekiah served God all his life. God blessed him.

Corresponding Music

The Singing Bible, Disc 3 – Track 5
Song Title: *"Oh, Israel Turn Back to God"*

The Time of the Kings

Fingerplay

Do the fingerplay *"This Little King"*. Focus on the sound and motion for the letter 'N'.

Key Idea: 'N' = tap top of hand twice with 2 fingers of other hand and say *N-N*

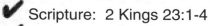

Bible Story

Read the Bible story from **one** of the following resources:

✔ Scripture: 2 Kings 23:1-4

✔ *A Child's First Bible* p. 130-131

✔ *The New Bible in Pictures for Little Eyes* p. 204-205

Key Idea: Josiah followed God's rules.

Devotional Activity

Read and discuss the devotion from **one** of the following resources:

✔ *Big Thoughts for Little People*
Read the two pages for letter 'N'.

✔ *Teach Them to Your Children*
Read the two pages for letter 'N'.

✔ *My ABC Bible Verses*
Read the two pages for letter 'N'.

Key Idea: Share a devotional focusing on character traits or memory work based on the letter 'N'.

Letter Activity

Use masking tape to make a large 'N' on the floor. Have students place blocks on the tape to trace the letter. Each time a block is placed on the tape, students make the letter **sound**.

Key Idea: Each letter has a name and a sound, just like animals do. For example, a bunny may be named Cottontail, but it makes the sound, *Squeak.*

Bible Activity

Give each student a piece of paper. Help students complete each of the following directions one at a time:

Draw 2 blue circles at the top of the page to be Josiah's eyes. Draw a black square in the center of the page to be a Bible. Draw a red smile at the bottom of the page.

Key Idea: King Josiah read God's book. He told others to do what it said in God's book.

Corresponding Music

The Singing Bible, Disc 3 – Track 5
Song Title: *"Oh, Israel Turn Back to God"*

The Time of the Kings

Fingerplay

Do the fingerplay *"This Little King"*. Focus on the sound and motion for the letter 'N'.

<u>Key Idea</u>: 'N' = tap top of hand twice with 2 fingers of other hand and say *N-N*

Letter Activity

Write a big 'N' on a piece of paper. Have students use fingerpaints, paints and paintbrushes, or playdough to fill in the letter.

<u>Key Idea</u>: Students will become familiar with the shape and appearance of the capital letter 'N'.

Bible Story

Read the Bible story from **one** of the following resources:

 Scripture: Ezra 9:9-10, 13-14

 *A Child's First Bible* p. 146-147

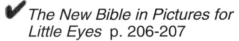 *The New Bible in Pictures for Little Eyes* p. 206-207

<u>Key Idea</u>: The people rebuilt the temple and changed their ways.

Bible Activity

Say, *The people of Israel disobeyed God and were punished. Have you ever disobeyed? What did you do that was wrong? God forgave the people and gave them another chance to do what was right. Have you ever been forgiven? What should you do when you have been forgiven? Let's pray and thank God for forgiving our sins.*

<u>Key Idea</u>: God forgave the Israelites for their sins and expected them to change their ways and do what was right.

Dramatic Play

Use a transparent container with a lid. Add the following items to symbolize things people worship: a marble as the sun, a Lego person as a king, a small plastic animal as a statue, and coins as money. Add oats, cornmeal, bird seed, or rice to hide the items. Tape the lid shut. Have students turn the container and each time they see an object say, *No! No! Worship only God.*

<u>Key Idea</u>: Ezra helped Israel turn back to God and worship only God.

Corresponding Music

The Singing Bible, Disc 3 – Track 5
Song Title: *"Oh, Israel Turn Back to God"*

The Time of the Kings

Fingerplay

Do the fingerplay *"This Little King"*. Focus on the sound and motion for the letter 'N'.

<u>Key Idea</u>: 'N' = tap top of hand twice with 2 fingers of other hand and say *N-N*

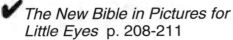

Bible Story

Read the Bible story from **one** of the following resources:

✔ Scripture: Job 2:3-10; 42:10

✔ *A Child's First Bible* p. 78-79

✔ *The New Bible in Pictures for Little Eyes* p. 208-211

<u>Key Idea</u>:   Job was tested.

Math Activity

Line up the following objects to show Job's possessions: a cereal piece for food, a block for a house, a coin for money, a cotton ball for sheep, and a play person for a child. Have students count the objects. Remove objects one at a time and have students recount each time. When none are left, explain zero. Add objects back one at a time and have students recount each time.

<u>Key Idea</u>:   Satan took away all Job had, but Job stayed faithful to God.

Letter Activity

Use the 'N' flashcard from the Appendix. Have students trace the capital and small letter 'N's' on the flashcard with their fingers. Using the flashcard as a model, choose either sidewalk chalk or 2 crayons taped together and paper to write more 'N's'.

<u>Key Idea</u>:   Practice the motions needed to make the letter 'N'.

Bible Activity

Ask students, *What blessings has God given you?* Some possible blessings include the following: a house, a family, food, clothing, toys, friends, and a church.

Say to the students, *Have you ever had any blessings taken away? How did you feel? Did you get mad at God? What does God want us to do even when some of our blessings are taken away?*

<u>Key Idea</u>:   Job praised God when he was blessed and when he was hurting. Blessings come from God. Sad things come from Satan.

Corresponding Music

None this lesson

Isaiah and Jeremiah Are God's Friends

Fingerplay

Do the fingerplay *"Off They Go"*. Focus on the sound and motion for the letter 'O'.

<u>Key Idea</u>: 'O' = brush off one hand with the other hand and say *O-O*

Letter Activity

Copy the 'O' flashcard found in the Appendix. Show the letter side of the flashcard to the students. Read the *Hint* aloud. Demonstrate the motion and sound for 'O'. Have the students repeat it.

<u>Key Idea</u>: Students should eventually do the motion and say the sound for each flashcard without needing a *Hint* or a demonstration from you.

Bible Story

Read the Bible story from **one** of the following resources:

✔ Scripture: Isaiah 1:1-4; 2:8-9

✔ *The New Bible in Pictures for Little Eyes* p. 212-213

<u>Key Idea</u>: Isaiah warned the people.

Bible Activity

Give each student a piece of paper. Help students complete each of the following directions one at a time: Draw 2 black lines coming down from the top of the page to be God's voice. Write the letters, 'N', 'O' on the left side of the page. Draw and color a red circle on the right side of the page to be a stoplight. Draw 3 orange triangles at the bottom of the page to show fire.

<u>Key Idea</u>: God told the people that they were sinning and that they needed to stop. Otherwise, their city would be burned up.

Active Exploration

Talk about the 3 colors on a stoplight. Assign students one of the following actions to do: skip, hop, crawl, spin, flap arms to "fly", walk forward, walk backward, or tiptoe. If you say, *Green,* students do the action quickly. If you say, *Yellow,* students do the action very slowly. If you say, *Red,* students stand still. For younger students, hold up red, yellow, or green colored papers instead of calling out the colors.

<u>Key Idea</u>: Just like a stoplight protects us, God sent Isaiah to warn people to stop their sinful actions.

Corresponding Music

The Singing Bible, Disc 3 – Track 5
Song Title: *"Oh, Israel Turn Back to God"*

Fingerplay: Off They Go

Days 1-5

Isaiah whispers.	*Whisper this line of the fingerplay*
Isaiah shouts!	*Shout this line of the fingerplay*
The people run Isaiah off!	*Pump arms as if running*
O-O-Off!	*Brush one hand with the other*
God is sad.	*Pull fingers down face*
Isaiah points out.	*Point with index finger*
The people shut God's words off.	*Hold hands open, slam shut*
O-O-Off!	*Brush one hand with the other*
Jeremiah writes.	*Use finger to write on palm*
Jeremiah talks.	*Point to mouth*
The king runs Jeremiah off.	*Pump arms as if running*
O-O-Off!	*Brush one hand with the other*
The people are bad.	*Tap hand with two fingers*
The people must go.	*Point thumb over shoulder*
God teaches them	*Point up*
They need him so.	*Cross arms on chest*

Isaiah and Jeremiah Are God's Friends

Fingerplay

Do the fingerplay *"Off They Go"*. Focus on the sound and motion for the letter 'O'.

Key Idea: 'O' = brush off one hand with the other hand and say *O-O*

Bible Story

Read the Bible story from **one** of the following resources:

✔ Scripture: Isaiah 11:6-10

✔ *The New Bible in Pictures for Little Eyes* p. 214-215

Key Idea: Everything will be perfect.

Dramatic Play

Imitate an animal's movements and sounds, while students guess the name of that animal. Then, have students mimic those actions until you say, *Freeze.* Students freeze by holding their bodies in a pose that shows that animal. Repeat the activity using different animals. Possible ideas for animals include the following: lion, bear, lamb, cow, goat, snake, cat, and dog.

Key Idea: Someday all the animals will get along without hurting one another.

Letter Activity

Copy the *Hide and Seek 'O'* page. Have students circle, color, highlight, or point to the 'O's on the page. Younger students may need help in order to find any 'O's at all. It is not necessary to find all the 'O's. On the bottom of the page, have students connect 'O' to 'o' by tracing the dotted line from left to right.

Key Idea: Students should eventually recognize the capital and small letter 'O' within words.

Bible Activity

Copy *Count on Me* (in Appendix). Direct students to draw red smiles in each of the boxes. Younger students make 2 smiles in each box. Older students make 3 smiles in each box. Point to each smile as you count it. Write the numbers on the lines below each box as you count. Say the numbers below the boxes to count by 2's or by 3's (counting either '2', '4', '6'... or '3', '6', '9' ...).

Key Idea: God will make the world perfect again someday, when Christ returns to reign over all things.

Corresponding Music

None this lesson

Hide and Seek 'O'

God is sad.

Isaiah points out.

People shut

God's words off. O-O-Off!

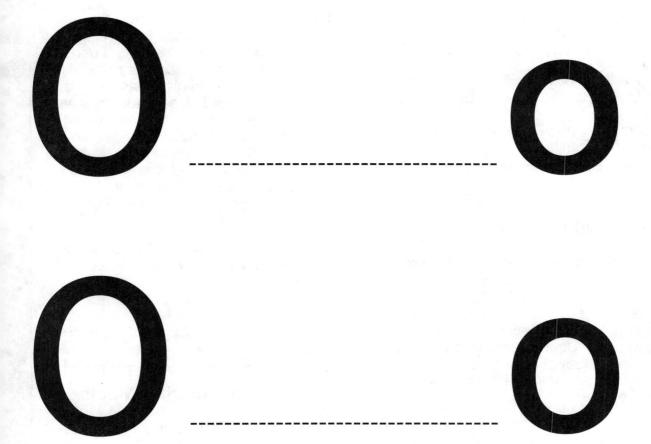

Isaiah and Jeremiah Are God's Friends

Fingerplay

Do the fingerplay *"Off They Go"*. Focus on the sound and motion for the letter 'O'.

Key Idea: 'O' = brush off one hand with the other hand and say *O-O*

Letter Activity

Write a big 'O' on a piece of paper. Have students glue cotton balls or pieces of yarn to the letter. Younger students will need you to apply drops of glue on the letter for them first.

Key Idea: Students will become familiar with the shape and appearance of the capital letter 'O'.

Bible Story

Read the Bible story from **one** of the following resources:

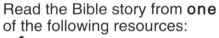 Scripture: Jeremiah 32:26-28, 32-34, 37-38

 *A Child's First Bible* p. 132-133

 *The New Bible in Pictures for Little Eyes* p. 216-217

Key Idea: The people didn't want to listen to Jeremiah.

Bible Activity

Act out the Bible story. Have the students be Jeremiah. Imitate the people in the story by saying, *I don't want to hear what God has to say.* Tell "Jeremiah" to hold his wrists together like they are tied. Designate an area as the prison. Have Jeremiah walk to the prison and fall down inside. Set up stuffed animals to be "people" outside the prison and have them point and laugh at Jeremiah. Tell Jeremiah to kneel and pray, ignoring the people.

Key Idea: Jeremiah did what God told him even when the people wouldn't listen.

Math Activity

Use masking tape to outline a square on the floor. Youngers: Set out objects of various sizes. Ask students which objects will fit inside the square. Olders: Set out objects that fit inside the square. Direct students to place a certain number of objects, or a particular object, inside or outside the square.

Key Idea: God is with us whether we are inside or outside.

Corresponding Music

The Singing Bible, Disc 3 – Track 5
Song Title: *"Oh, Israel Turn Back to God"*

Isaiah and Jeremiah Are God's Friends

Fingerplay

Do the fingerplay *"Off They Go"*. Focus on the sound and motion for the letter 'O'.

Key Idea: 'O' = brush off one hand with the other hand and say *O-O*

Bible Story

Read the Bible story from **one** of the following resources:

✔ Scripture: Jeremiah 36:1-3, 22-23

✔ *The New Bible in Pictures for Little Eyes* p. 218-221

Key Idea: The king burned the scroll.

Art Activity

Give each student a half sheet of regular **white paper** to be a scroll. Have students cover the sheet with **small pieces of masking tape** to give it an aged look. Older students may cut their own tape into small pieces. Provide **fingerpaint** for students to use to "paint writing" on the scroll. Fold up the ends of the scroll, so it is slightly rolled up.

Key Idea: God told Jeremiah what to write on the scroll.

Letter Activity

Use masking tape to make a large 'O' on the floor. Have students drive a toy car or other toy vehicle on the tape to trace the letter. Have students say the letter **sound** as they drive.

Key Idea: Each letter has a name and a sound, just like animals do. For example, a lamb may be named Whitey, but it makes the sound, *Baa.*

Bible Activity

Act out the Bible story. Have students be Jeremiah, and you be the bad king. Have Jeremiah sit down and pretend to write. Tell Jeremiah to get up and hand the scroll to you. Tear up the scroll and burn it in the fire. Have Jeremiah run and hide. You search for him, but God hides Jeremiah from you.

Key Idea: The scroll was a warning from God to the people. The king was punished for burning it.

Corresponding Music

The Singing Bible, Disc 3 – Track 5
Song Title: *"Oh, Israel Turn Back to God"*

Isaiah and Jeremiah Are God's Friends

Fingerplay

Do the fingerplay *"Off They Go"*. Focus on the sound and motion for the letter 'O'.

<u>Key Idea</u>: 'O' = brush off one hand with the other hand and say *O-O*

Bible Story

Read the Bible story from **one** of the following resources:

✔ Scripture: Jeremiah 34:1-3

✔ *The New Bible in Pictures for Little Eyes* p. 222-223

<u>Key Idea</u>: The Israelites were taken to Babylon.

Devotional Activity

Read and discuss the devotion from **one** of the following resources:

✔ *Big Thoughts for Little People*
Read the two pages for letter 'O'.

✔ *Teach Them to Your Children*
Read the two pages for letter 'O'.

✔ *My ABC Bible Verses*
Read the two pages for letter 'O'.

<u>Key Idea</u>: Share a devotional focusing on character traits or memory work based on the letter 'O'.

Letter Activity

Use the 'O' flashcard from the Appendix. Have students trace the capital and small letter 'O' on the flashcard with their fingers. Using the flashcard as a model, give students either a small amount of cooking oil or liquid soap on an aluminum pan or plate to use to write more 'O's'.

<u>Key Idea</u>: Practice the motions needed to make the letter 'O'.

Bible Activity

Explain to students that just like God didn't want to punish Israel, parents don't like to punish their children either. So, we need to make sure we are listening to God and working hard to follow his commands. Share some things you need to work on as an adult. Ask students, *What are some things you need to work on?* Pray with students for God to help each of you follow him better.

<u>Key Idea</u>: God gives us the Bible, so we know what He wants us to do.

Corresponding Music

The Singing Bible, Disc 3 – Track 5
Song Title: *"Oh, Israel Turn Back to God"*

Jonah Tries to Run

Fingerplay

Do the fingerplay *"One to Ten"*. Focus on the sound and motion for the letter 'P'.

Key Idea: 'P' = make fists with hands, pull in and say *P-P*

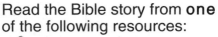

Bible Story

Read the Bible story from **one** of the following resources:

✔ Scripture: Jonah 1:1-3

✔ *A Child's First Bible* p. 126

✔ *The New Bible in Pictures for Little Eyes* p. 224-225

Key Idea: Jonah disobeyed God.

Math Activity

Use blocks to build a simple city to represent Ninevah. Have students duplicate the city with their own blocks. Next, assign students an action to perform as they pretend to be Jonah going away from the city. Possible actions include the following: tiptoe, crawl, hop, spin, walk slowly, take huge steps, walk backward, and step sideways.

Key Idea: Jonah ran away from Ninevah, but he couldn't run away from God.

Letter Activity

Copy the 'P' flashcard found in the Appendix. Show the letter side of the flashcard to the students. Read the *Hint* aloud. Demonstrate the motion and sound for 'P'. Have the students repeat it.

Key Idea: Students should eventually do the motion and say the sound for each flashcard without needing a *Hint* or a demonstration from you.

Bible Activity

Give each student a piece of paper. Help students complete each of the following directions one at a time: Draw a brown path starting at the top of the page. Continue drawing the path and make it curve to the left and then to the right. Have the path end at the bottom of the page. Draw a blue, wavy line at the bottom of the page to be water.

Key Idea: God gave Jonah a job to do, but Jonah disobeyed. He went down a different path and got on a boat.

Corresponding Music

The Singing Bible, Disc 3 – Track 8
Song Title: *"Jonah and the Whale"*

Fingerplay: One to Ten

Days 1-5

As I say one,	*Hold up 1 finger*
Jonah packs and runs.	*Run in place*
As I say two,	*Hold up 2 fingers*
The wind says *Woo-Hoo.*	*Blow and sway back and forth*
As I say three,	*Hold up 3 fingers*
The boat rocks in the sea.	*Hug self and rock back and forth*
As I say four,	*Hold up 4 fingers*
Men *P-Pull* the oars.	*Grab with fists and pull toward self*
As I say five,	*Hold up 5 fingers*
Jonah's pitched off the side.	*Jump*
As I say six,	*Hold up 6 fingers*
Jonah's swallowed by a fish.	*Roll into a ball, hug knees*
As I say seven,	*Hold up 7 fingers*
Jonah prays to heaven.	*Fold hands and kneel*
As I say eight,	*Hold up 8 fingers*
The fish gives a shake.	*Shake body*
As I say nine,	*Hold up 9 fingers*
Jonah's feeling fine.	*Jump up and down waving hands*
As I say ten,	*Hold up 10 fingers,*
Jonah listens to God again.	*Cup hand to ear*

Jonah Tries to Run

Fingerplay

Do the fingerplay *"One to Ten"*. Focus on the sound and motion for the letter 'P'.

Key Idea: 'P' = make fists with hands, pull in and say *P-P*

Letter Activity

Use masking tape to make a large 'P' on the floor. Have students tiptoe on the tape to trace the letter. Then, have students jump off the end of the letter saying the letter **sound** as they jump.

Key Idea: Each letter has a name and a sound, just like animals do. For example, a bird may be named Robin, but it makes the sound, *Chirp.*

Bible Story

Read the Bible story from **one** of the following resources:

 Scripture: Jonah 1:4, 11-12, 15-17

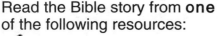 *A Child's First Bible* p. 126

 *The New Bible in Pictures for Little Eyes* p. 226-227

Key Idea: God sent a storm.

Bible Activity

Act out the Bible story. Have students pretend to be Jonah on the boat rocking back and forth while you make these sound effects: blow to make windy sounds, tap hands on legs for rain, and clap for lightning.

Now, have Jonah splash into the water and make wild motions with his hands and feet. Say, *Gulp!* Have Jonah sit inside the fish with his arms wrapped around his legs. Tell Jonah to kneel and pray.

Key Idea: Jonah knew he had disobeyed God and that God was punishing him.

Art Activity

Give each student a piece of **white paper**. Help students place their shoe on the paper and trace around it with a **black marker** to make a whale. Have students color the whale with **crayons**. Students may also draw and color other things in their ocean scenes. Last, have students color over all of their crayon drawings with purple, blue, and green **watercolor markers**.

Key Idea: God sent the storm and the whale to help Jonah obey him.

Corresponding Music

The Singing Bible, Disc 3 – Track 8
Song Title: *"Jonah and the Whale"*

Jonah Tries to Run

Fingerplay

Do the fingerplay *"One to Ten"*. Focus on the sound and motion for the letter 'P'.

Key Idea: 'P' = make fists with hands, pull in and say *P-P*

Bible Story

Reread the Bible story from day 2 in **one** of the following resources:

✔ Scripture: Jonah 1:4, 11-12, 15-17

✔ *A Child's First Bible* p. 126

✔ *The New Bible in Pictures for Little Eyes* p. 226-227

Key Idea: God sent a storm.

Active Exploration

Set out items such as a tissue, a pencil, a paper clip, a cotton ball, a block, and a heavy toy. Put the items one at a time on a tabletop or other smooth surface. Have students be a storm blowing each item across the "water". See which items move the farthest, and which items are not moved by the storm.

Key Idea: God sent a huge storm to show Jonah that God knew where Jonah was hiding.

Letter Activity

Copy the *Hide and Seek 'P'* page. Have students circle, color, highlight, or point to the 'P's' on the page. Younger students may need help in order to find any 'P's' at all. It is not necessary to find all the 'P's'. On the bottom of the page, have students connect 'P' to 'p' by tracing the dotted line from left to right.

Key Idea: Students should eventually recognize the capital and small letter 'P' within words.

Bible Activity

Copy *Count on Me* (in Appendix). Direct students to draw fish by making orange oval bodies with triangle tails in each of the boxes. Younger students make 2 fish in each box. Older students make 3 fish in each box. Point to each fish as you count it. Write the numbers on the lines below each box as you count. Say the numbers below the boxes to count by 2's or by 3's (counting either '2', '4', '6'... or '3', '6', '9' ...).

Key Idea: God sent a fish to save Jonah.

Corresponding Music

The Singing Bible, Disc 3 – Track 8
Song Title: *"Jonah and the Whale"*

Hide and Seek 'P'

As I say four,

Men p-pull the oars.

As I say five,

Jonah's pitched off the side.

P... P... P...

P ----------------------------- p

P ----------------------------- p

Jonah Tries to Run

Fingerplay

Do the fingerplay *"One to Ten".* Focus on the sound and motion for the letter 'P'.

Key Idea: 'P' = make fists with hands, pull in and say *P-P*

Letter Activity

Write a big 'P' on a piece of paper. Have students glue dried macaroni or raisins to the letter. Younger students will need you to apply drops of glue on the letter for them first.

Key Idea: Students will become familiar with the shape and appearance of the capital letter 'P'.

Bible Story

Read the Bible story from **one** of the following resources:

✔ Scripture: Jonah 2:10; 3:1-5, 10

✔ *A Child's First Bible* p. 127

✔ *The New Bible in Pictures for Little Eyes* p. 228-229

Key Idea: Jonah did what God said.

Bible Activity

Have students give directions to their stuffed animals. Students need to help their animals listen and obey, just like the Ninevites listened to God's warning. Some possible directions students could give include the following: clap your paws, lay on your back, stand on your head, jump up and down, touch your feet, bow down, spin around, and wave good-bye.

Tell students that we need to listen to the warnings God gives us in the Bible.

Key Idea: God saved Ninevah because the Ninevites listened to Jonah's warning from God.

Dramatic Play

Have students pretend to be the fish that swallowed Jonah and use a laundry basket for the land. The students toss a rolled up pair of socks or a beanbag toward the basket, to show Jonah being spit out. The goal is to get the socks or beanbag into the basket. After each toss, say, *Jonah go to Ninevah.* Use positional words such as beside, in, out, next to, far away, and near to describe where each toss lands.

Key Idea: God created everything. Even the fish had to obey God.

Corresponding Music

The Singing Bible, Disc 3 – Track 8
Song Title: *"Jonah and the Whale"*

Jonah Tries to Run

Fingerplay

Do the fingerplay *"One to Ten"*. Focus on the sound and motion for the letter 'P'.

<u>Key Idea:</u> 'P' = make fists with hands, pull in and say *P-P*

Bible Story

Reread the Bible story from day 4 in **one** of the following resources:

✔ Scripture: Jonah 2:10; 3:1-5, 10

✔ *A Child's First Bible* p. 127

✔ *The New Bible in Pictures for Little Eyes* p. 228-229

<u>Key Idea:</u> Jonah did what God said.

Devotional Activity

Read and discuss the devotion from **one** of the following resources:

✔ *Big Thoughts for Little People*
Read the two pages for letter 'P'.

✔ *Teach Them to Your Children*
Read the two pages for letter 'P'.

✔ *My ABC Bible Verses*
Read the two pages for letter 'P'.

<u>Key Idea:</u> Share a devotional focusing on character traits or memory work based on the letter 'P'.

Letter Activity

Use the 'P' flashcard from the Appendix. Have students trace the capital and small letter 'P' on the flashcard with their fingers. Using the flashcard as a model, choose either pudding, chocolate syrup, baby food, or fingerpaint on a plate, pan, or piece of paper for students to write more 'P's'.

<u>Key Idea:</u> Practice the motions needed to make the letter 'P'.

Bible Activity

Have students share kind things they can do for others because of God's love for us. Some simple ideas that show kindness include giving a hug, being cheerful, praying for others, helping others, speaking in a kind voice, letting others go first, complimenting others, giving offering at church, and doing a task without being asked.

<u>Key Idea:</u> When we love God, we will want to share that love with others by being kind.

Corresponding Music

The Singing Bible, Disc 3 – Track 8
Song Title: *"Jonah and the Whale"*

Daniel Is Loyal to God

Fingerplay

Do the fingerplay *"What Do You Know?"* Focus on reviewing the sounds and motions for the letters.

Key Idea: Practice the sounds and motions for the letters 'A-P'.

Bible Story

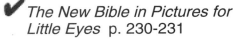

Read the Bible story from **one** of the following resources:

✔ Scripture: Daniel 1:3-5, 8, 17

✔ *A Child's First Bible* p. 134-135

✔ *The New Bible in Pictures for Little Eyes* p. 230-231

Key Idea: Daniel went to Babylon.

Math Activity

Youngers: Set out plastic plates with play food on each plate. Have students count the pieces of food on each plate. After counting, students say, *Take it away,* to mimic Daniel.
Olders: Write numbers on index cards. Set out plates and place one card on each plate. Have students put pieces of food on each plate to match the number on the card. After counting students say, *Take it away.*

Key Idea: Daniel served God, so he chose not to eat the king's food.

Letter Activity

This is a review week. Review all the flashcards from the previous weeks. Show the letter side of each flashcard to the students. Have them respond with the motion and sound. If needed, read the *Hint* or demonstrate the motion and sound.

Key Idea: Students should eventually do the motion and say the sound for each flashcard without needing a *Hint* or a demonstration from you.

Bible Activity

Copy *Count on Me* (in Appendix). Direct students to draw grapes by making purple circles in the each of the boxes. Younger students make 2 grapes in each box. Older students make 3 grapes in each box. Point to each grape as you count it with the students. Write the numbers on the lines below each box as you count. Say the numbers below the boxes to count by 2's or by 3's (counting either '2', '4', '6'... or '3', '6', '9' ...).

Key Idea: Daniel honored God with what he chose to eat and drink.

Corresponding Music

None this lesson

Fingerplay: What Do You Know?

We've learned about *A-A-Adam*	*Hands on cheeks in surprise*
And *B-B-Boat,*	*Hug yourself and rock side-to-side*
C-C-Clippity clop	*Tap palms on thighs in rhythm*
And *D-D-Dusty* camel.	*Hold reins; move up and down*
E-E-Empty jars	*Shake hand to shake empty jar*
And *F-F-Fire,*	*Wiggle 10 fingers like flames*
G-G-Gurgle	*Hold nose, put hand up*
And *H-H-Helping* hands.	*Lace fingers, move up and down*
I-Impossible	*Push palms up as if lifting*
And *J-J-Joyful* jumping,	*2 fingers jump on palm of hand*
K-K-clapping hands	*Clap hands above head*
And *L-L-La-La-La.*	*Swing hand back and forth*
M-M-Miracles	*Pat hand over mouth, pull it away*
And *N-N-Naughty* king,	*Tap top of hand with 2 fingers*
O-O-Off	*Brush one hand with the other*
And *P-P-Pulling* oars.	*Make fists and pull them in*
Now, as Daniel	*Bow head*
Prays to God,	*Fold hands to pray*
God saves Daniel	*Point up*
From the lions' mouths.	*Snap teeth together*
Just like the others	*Open palms together like Bible*
God has plans for you too.	*Point up, then point to yourself*
Never forget	*Shake head, "No"*
What God can do!	*Spread arms wide*

Daniel Is Loyal to God

Fingerplay

Do the fingerplay *"What Do You Know?"* Focus on reviewing the sounds and motions for the letters.

Key Idea: Practice the sounds and motions for the letters 'A-P'.

Bible Story

Read the Bible story from **one** of the following resources:

 Scripture: Daniel 5:3-6, 12, 26-28

 *A Child's First Bible* p. 140-141

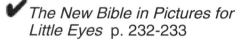 *The New Bible in Pictures for Little Eyes* p. 232-233

Key Idea: The writing on the wall warned the king.

Active Exploration

Put a sheet of brightly colored paper in the bottom of a pan or cookie sheet. Pour rice, cornmeal, salt, or oatmeal in a layer on top of the paper. Have students use their fingers to write letters or numbers and draw pictures in the pan, just like the hand wrote on the wall in the story. Have students tell you about their "drawings".

Key Idea: The king called Daniel to read the writing on the wall. God told Daniel what it meant.

Letter Activity

Copy the *Hide-n-Seek Review* page. Choose a letter from 'M-P' to review. Have students circle, color, highlight, or point to the chosen letter. Younger students may need help in order to find any of the chosen letters. On the bottom of the page, have students draw a line to connect each capital letter to its matching lowercase letter.

Key Idea: Students should eventually recognize the capital and small letters 'M-P' within words.

Bible Activity

Give each student a piece of paper. Help students complete each of the following directions one at a time: Trace around your hand in the middle of the page. Next, let's practice writing some letters. Write a 'C' above the hand. Write a 'J' on the left side of the hand. Write an 'L' on the right side of the hand. Write an 'O' below the hand.

Key Idea: A hand wrote on the wall at the king's party to tell the king God was taking his kingdom from him.

Corresponding Music

None this lesson

Hide and Seek Review

We've learned about M-M-Miracles

And N-N-Naughty king,

O-O-off,

And P-P-Pulling oars.

M

N

O

P

p

o

n

m

Daniel Is Loyal to God

Fingerplay

Do the fingerplay *"What Do You Know?"* Focus on reviewing the sounds and motions for the letters.

Key Idea: Practice the sounds and motions for the letters 'A-P'.

Bible Story

Read the Bible story from **one** of the following resources:

✔ Scripture: Daniel 6:3, 11-14

✔ *A Child's First Bible* p. 142

✔ *The New Bible in Pictures for Little Eyes* p. 234-235

Key Idea: Daniel kept praying.

Dramatic Play

Youngers: Hide a stuffed animal somewhere in the room. Ask students to find the stuffed animal. Limit the search to one room. You may give hints about the animal's hiding place. Olders: Play hide and seek. Limit the hiding area, so students remain safe in their choice of hiding places. Take turns hiding and counting to 10. The seeker tiptoes to find the hider.

Key Idea: The men hid to catch Daniel praying. Daniel kept praying.

Letter Activity

Choose one letter from 'A-P' to review. Write that letter on a big piece of paper. Use water to thin glue and have students "paint" the glue on the letter. Then, sprinkle either salt, coffee grounds, glitter, or any kind of spice on the glue. Younger students will need you to help them with the sprinkling part.

Key Idea: Students will become familiar with the shape and appearance of the capital letters.

Bible Activity

Act out the Bible story. You be the king, have students be Daniel, and set up stuffed animals to be men watching Daniel. Read the law that no one may pray to anyone except you (the king), or they will be put in the lions' den. Have Daniel kneel and pray to God. Have the "men" point to Daniel and sneak off one by one to tell you. Say, *I don't want to put Daniel with the lions.*

Key Idea: The kings' men wanted to get rid of Daniel, but Daniel prayed for God to take care of him.

Corresponding Music

The Singing Bible, Disc 3 – Track 7
Song Title: *"Daniel"*

Daniel Is Loyal to God

Fingerplay

Do the fingerplay *"What Do You Know?"* Focus on reviewing the sounds and motions for the letters.

<u>Key Idea</u>: Practice the sounds and motions for the letters 'A-P'.

Bible Story

Reread the Bible story from day 3 in **one** of the following resources:

✔ Scripture: Daniel 6:3, 11-14

✔ *A Child's First Bible* p. 142

✔ *The New Bible in Pictures for Little Eyes* p. 234-235

<u>Key Idea</u>: Daniel kept praying.

Devotional Activity

Read and discuss the devotion from **one** of the following resources:

✔ *Big Thoughts for Little People*
Review verses for 'M', 'N', 'O', 'P'

✔ *Teach Them to Your Children*
Review verses for 'M', 'N', 'O', 'P'

✔ *My ABC Bible Verses*
Review verses for 'M', 'N', 'O', 'P'

<u>Key Idea</u>: Share a devotional focusing on character traits or memory work based on the letters 'M', 'N', 'O', 'P'.

Letter Activity

Choose one or more of the flashcards from the previous weeks to review. Have students trace the capital and small letters on the flashcards with their fingers. Using the flashcards as models, choose either markers and markerboards or pieces of carpet and fingers to practice writing more letters.

<u>Key Idea</u>: Practice the motions needed to make the letters.

Bible Activity

Direct students to practice saying, *I like you,* to a special toy in a variety of voices. Voices for students to use include a silly voice, an angry voice, a high voice, a low voice, and a laughing voice.

Discuss what kind of voice shows the toy it is very special. Have students practice using that voice. Point out that we should talk to God using our special voice because He is so holy.

<u>Key Idea</u>: God is very special, and we should treat him that way.

Corresponding Music

The Singing Bible, Disc 3 – Track 7
Song Title: *"Daniel"*

Daniel Is Loyal to God

Fingerplay

Do the fingerplay *"What Do You Know?"* Focus on reviewing the sounds and motions for the letters.

<u>Key Idea</u>: Practice the sounds and motions for the letters 'A-P'.

Letter Activity

Choose one or more of the letters 'A-P' to review. Use masking tape to make the large review letter on the floor. Have students sit on a pillow and scoot on the tape to trace the letter. Have students say the letter **sound** as they scoot.

<u>Key Idea</u>: Each letter has a name and a sound, just like animals do. For example, a duck may be named Ducky, but it makes the sound, *Quack.*

Bible Story

Read the Bible story from **one** of the following resources:

 Scripture: Daniel 6:16, 19-23

 A Child's First Bible p. 142-143

 The New Bible in Pictures for Little Eyes p. 236-237

<u>Key Idea</u>: God saved Daniel from the lions.

Bible Activity

Act out the Bible story. You be Daniel, have the students be angels, and set out props to be lions in the den. Kneel and pray to ask God to protect you from the lions.

Have students tiptoe into the den, going from "lion to lion" touching their mouths. Have students lay each lion down on its back. Pray and thank God for his protection.

<u>Key Idea</u>: God heard Daniel's prayer and sent angels to protect Daniel from the lions.

Art Activity

Give each student a **paper plate** or a white circle cut out of paper to be a lion's head. Have students **color** the circle orange, yellow, and brown like a lion. On the lion's head draw eyes, a nose, whiskers, and a <u>closed</u> mouth. Last, have students use their **scissors** to make snips all around the edge of the circle to create a lion's mane. Bend the mane, so it sticks out.

<u>Key Idea</u>: God shut the lions' mouths, so they did not hurt Daniel.

Corresponding Music

The Singing Bible, Disc 3 – Track 7
Song Title: *"Daniel"*

Jesus' Birth

Fingerplay

Do the fingerplay *"One Special Baby"*. Focus on the sound and motion for the letter 'Q'.

<u>Key Idea</u>: 'Q' = shake whole body, as if quivering and say *Q-Q*

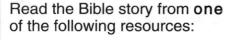
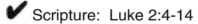

Bible Story

Read the Bible story from **one** of the following resources:

✔ Scripture: Luke 2:4-14
✔ *A Child's First Bible* p. 154-157
✔ *The New Bible in Pictures for Little Eyes* p. 240-241

<u>Key Idea</u>: Jesus was born.

Devotional Activity

Read and discuss the devotion from **one** of the following resources:

✔ *Big Thoughts for Little People*
Read the two pages for letter 'Q'.

✔ *Teach Them to Your Children*
Read the two pages for letter 'Q'.

✔ *My ABC Bible Verses*
Read the two pages for letter 'Q'.

<u>Key Idea</u>: Share a devotional focusing on character traits or memory work based on the letters 'Q'.

Letter Activity

Copy the 'Q' flashcard found in the Appendix. Show the letter side of the flashcard to the students. Read the Hint aloud. Demonstrate the motion and sound for 'Q'. Have the students repeat it.

<u>Key Idea</u>: Students should eventually do the motion and say the sound for each flashcard without needing a *Hint* or a demonstration from you.

Bible Activity

Copy the *YELLOW is...* page. Have students find yellow items in a magazine or a catalog to cut out. Use a marker to circle, box, or outline the yellow items, so that students have a line to follow as they cut.

Have students glue the items on the *YELLOW is...* page. Save this page. A page will be added each week to make a color book.

<u>Key Idea</u>: Yellow is for the bright light that shone from heaven as the angels sang about Jesus' birth. Jesus was born in Bethlehem.

Corresponding Music

The Singing Bible, Disc 4 – Track 1
Song Title: *"Starry Sky"*

Fingerplay: One Special Baby

Days 1-5

One special baby	*Hold up 1 finger*
Born this quiet night.	*Rest head on 2 hands*
Angels sing praises	*Swing hand back and forth*
Shepherds *Q-Quiver* in fright.	*Shake whole body*
Two hold Jesus	*Hold up 2 fingers*
In a stable bare.	*Rub arms with hands*
Shepherds quickly come	*Pump arms back and forth*
To see the Lord there.	*Shade eyes with hand*
Three wise men travel	*Hold up 3 fingers*
With gifts quite far.	*Hold reins, move up and down*
So, come on spread the news.	*Sweep arms out*
Jesus is born!	*Reach arms up to heaven*

YELLOW is...

for the bright light from heaven
that shone as the angels sang about Jesus' birth.

Jesus' Birth

Fingerplay

Do the fingerplay *"One Special Baby"*. Focus on the sound and motion for the letter 'Q'.

Key Idea: 'Q' = shake whole body, as if quivering and say *Q-Q*

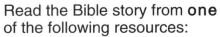

Bible Story

Read the Bible story from **one** of the following resources:

✔ Scripture: Luke 2:15-18

✔ *A Child's First Bible* p. 158-159

✔ *The New Bible in Pictures for Little Eyes* p. 242-243

Key Idea: Shepherds visited Jesus.

Art Activity

On **brown paper** draw the outline of a stable in **permanent marker**. Trace the outline with a thick line of **glue**. Have students follow these steps: Lay **dry spaghetti** or **toothpicks** on the glue lines. Glue **macaroni** or pieces of spaghetti on the stable floor to be straw. Glue two **cotton balls** on the straw as sheep. Glue a piece of **paper towel** on the straw to be Jesus.

Key Idea: The shepherds saw Jesus in the stable and worshiped him.

Letter Activity

Use masking tape to make a large 'Q' on the floor. Have students walk a stuffed animal on the tape to trace the letter. Then, have students walk the letter themselves, saying the letter **sound** as they walk.

Key Idea: Each letter has a name and a sound, just like animals do. For example, a frog may be named Slimy, but it makes the sound, *Ribbit.*

Bible Activity

Use props to set up the scene of Jesus' birth. Set out objects to represent the barn animals, Mary, Joseph, and baby Jesus. Have the students be the shepherds that find baby Jesus in the stable. The shepherds bow down and sing *"Happy Birthday"* to Jesus. Say a prayer of thanks to God for sending Jesus to be born on earth.

Key Idea: After the shepherds saw Jesus, they spread the news of his birth to everyone they met.

Corresponding Music

The Singing Bible, Disc 4 – Track 1
Song Title: *"Starry Sky"*

Jesus' Birth

Fingerplay

Do the fingerplay *"One Special Baby"*. Focus on the sound and motion for the letter 'Q'.

<u>Key Idea:</u> 'Q' = shake whole body, as if quivering and say *Q-Q*

Bible Story

Read the Bible story from **one** of the following resources:

✔ Scripture: Matthew 2:1-2, 9-10

✔ *A Child's First Bible* p. 162

✔ *The New Bible in Pictures for Little Eyes* p. 244-245

<u>Key Idea:</u> Magi followed God's star.

Math Activity

On paper, draw the following items: line, 'X', zig-zag, circle, oval, triangle, square, rectangle, and star. Leave space next to each item for the students to copy it. For younger students, make dotted outlines of the items to trace instead. Then, draw different shapes on several cards and tape them to the floor. Have students find those shapes in their surroundings, point them out, and run to the card with the same shape.

<u>Key Idea:</u> The magi found a star that led them to Jesus.

Letter Activity

Copy the *Hide and Seek 'Q'* page. Have students circle, color, highlight, or point to the 'Q's' on the page. Younger students may need help in finding any 'Q's' at all. It is not necessary to find all the 'Q's'. On the bottom of the page, have students connect 'Q' to 'q' by tracing the dotted line from left to right.

<u>Key Idea:</u> Students should eventually recognize the capital and small letter 'Q' within words.

Bible Activity

Copy *Count on Me* (in Appendix). Direct students to draw stars by making either yellow 5-point stars or yellow circles in the boxes. Younger students make 3 stars in each box. Older students make 4 stars in each box. Point to each star as you count it. Write the numbers on the lines below each box as you count. Say the numbers below the boxes to count by 3's or by 4's (counting either '3', '6', '9' ... or '4', '8', '12' ...).

<u>Key Idea:</u> The magi followed God's star to the place where baby Jesus was born.

Corresponding Music

The Singing Bible, Disc 4 – Track 1
Song Title: *"Starry Sky"*

Hide and Seek 'Q'

One special baby

Born this quiet night.

Angels sing praises

Shepherds Q-Q-Quiver in fright.

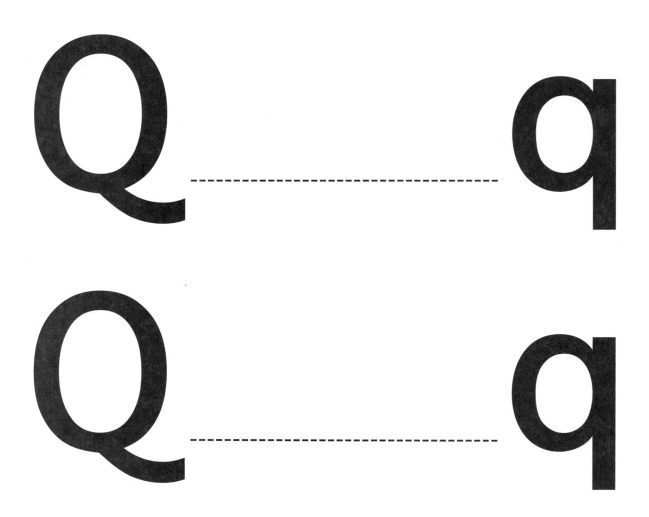

Jesus' Birth

Fingerplay

Do the fingerplay *"One Special Baby"*. Focus on the sound and motion for the letter 'Q'.

Key Idea: 'Q' = shake whole body, as if quivering and say *Q-Q*

Letter Activity

Write a big 'Q' on a piece of paper. Have students glue dry 'O'-shaped cereal or dried beans to the letter. Younger students will need you to apply drops of glue on the letter for them first.

Key Idea: Students will become familiar with the shape and appearance of the capital letter 'Q'.

Bible Story

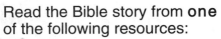

Read the Bible story from **one** of the following resources:

✔ Scripture: Matthew 2:11
✔ *A Child's First Bible* p. 163
✔ *The New Bible in Pictures for Little Eyes* p. 246-247

Key Idea: The magi saw Jesus.

Bible Activity

Have students talk about some of their favorite gifts they have received. Ask students to share why they received the gift. Say to the students, *Why did the magi give Jesus gifts? Why were the gifts so special? What are some "gifts" you can give back to Jesus?*

Some possible ideas of gifts to give back to Jesus include the following: praying respectfully, singing praises, listening to Bible stories, learning more about Jesus, and giving offering at church.

Key Idea: Jesus is God's gift to us.

Dramatic Play

Hide a baby doll or a present to represent Jesus, God's gift to us. Students are the magi searching to find Jesus. Sing or clap while the magi search for Jesus. As the magi get closer to Jesus, sing or clap more loudly. As the magi get farther away from Jesus, sing or clap more softly. After the magi find Jesus, they should kneel down and say, *Thank you God for your Son.* Take turns hiding and finding Jesus.

Key Idea: The magi found Jesus, gave gifts, and worshiped him.

Corresponding Music

The Singing Bible, Disc 4 – Track 1
Song Title: *"Starry Sky"*

Jesus' Birth

Fingerplay

Do the fingerplay *"One Special Baby"*. Focus on the sound and motion for the letter 'Q'.

Key Idea: 'Q' = shake whole body, as if quivering and say *Q-Q*

Bible Story

Read the Bible story from **one** of the following resources:

✔ Scripture: Luke 2:25-32

✔ *A Child's First Bible* p. 160-161

✔ *The New Bible in Pictures for Little Eyes* p. 248-249

Key Idea: Simeon saw Jesus.

Active Exploration

Take turns covering part of a doll or stuffed animal with a folded cloth. Take turns removing the cloth and uncovering the hidden body part. Say, *Peek-a-boo, I see a _____.* (For the blank, name the body part that was uncovered.) Possible body parts to cover include the eyes, nose, mouth, ears, hands, feet, arms, legs, knees, stomach, back, and head.

Key Idea: Simeon was so glad to see Jesus. Did you get to see your "baby" too?

Letter Activity

Use the 'Q' flashcard from the Appendix. Have students trace the capital and small letter 'Q's' on the flashcard with their fingers. Using the flashcard as a model, choose either a bar of soap on a mirror or an ice cube on construction paper to write more 'Q's'.

Key Idea: Practice the motions needed to make the letter 'Q'.

Bible Activity

Have students be Simeon. They may ask permission to hold baby Jesus.

As students pretend to hold baby Jesus have them perform the following actions: gently rock him in their arms, stroke his face, sing or hum to him, hug him gently, pat his back, and say a thank you prayer to God for sending baby Jesus to earth.

Key Idea: Simeon had been waiting to see Jesus. God had told Simeon he would see Jesus before Simeon died.

Corresponding Music

None this lesson

Jesus Grows Up and Begins His Ministry

Fingerplay

Do the fingerplay *"Jesus Is the Son of God"*. Focus on the sound and motion for the letter 'R'.

Key Idea: 'R' = hold chin with hand as if thinking and say *R-R*

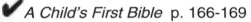

Bible Story

Read the Bible story from **one** of the following resources:

✔ Scripture: Luke 2:42-43, 46-47, 52

✔ *A Child's First Bible* p. 166-169

✔ *The New Bible in Pictures for Little Eyes* p. 250-251

Key Idea: Jesus was at the temple.

Art Activity

Give each student a piece of **colored construction paper**. Trace each student's hand and foot on the piece of paper. Older students may cut out the hand and foot shapes. Have students glue on 'O'-shaped cereal to fill in the hand and foot shapes. Apply dots of glue to the shapes first for the younger students.

Key Idea: Jesus was once a child. He had to grow up, just as the students have to grow up too.

Letter Activity

Copy the 'R' flashcard found in the Appendix. Show the letter side of the flashcard to the students. Read the *Hint* aloud. Demonstrate the motion and sound for 'R'. Have the students repeat it.

Key Idea: Students should eventually do the motion and say the sound for each flashcard without needing a *Hint* or a demonstration from you.

Bible Activity

Help students show some of the things they know. Some possible ideas include the following: point to objects and name the color of each object, count several items, walk, spin, somersault, jump, sing *"The Alphabet Song"*, hold up fingers to represent their age, and say a memory verse they know.

Key Idea: Even though Jesus was only a boy, He knew as much as the grown-ups at the temple.

Corresponding Music

None this lesson

Fingerplay: Jesus Is the Son of God
(Sing to the tune of *"Here We Go Round the Mulberry Bush"*)

Days 1-5

Jesus our Lord is always right,	*Marching*
Always right,	*Marching*
Always right.	*Marching*
Jesus our Lord is always right.	*Marching*
He is the Son of God!	*Point up*
Jesus is baptized in the river,	*Stand up, bend knees*
In the river,	*Stand up*
In the river,	*Bend knees*
Jesus is baptized in the river.	*Stand up, bend knees*
He is the Son of God!	*Stand up and point up*
Jesus replies, *No,* to Satan,	*Hands on hips, lean forward*
No, to Satan,	*Hands on hips, stand straight*
No, to Satan.	*Hands on hips, lean forward*
Jesus replies, *No,* to Satan.	*Hands on hips, lean forward*
I am the Son of God!	*Stand straight and point up*
Jesus is *r-r-ready* to pick his helpers,	*Hold chin with hand, thinking*
Pick his helpers,	*Shake someone's hand*
Pick his helpers.	*Shake someone's hand*
Jesus is *r-r-ready* to pick his helpers.	*Hold chin with hand, thinking*
He is the Son of God!	*Point up*

Jesus Grows Up and Begins His Ministry

Fingerplay

Do the fingerplay *"Jesus Is the Son of God"*. Focus on the sound and motion for the letter 'R'.

Key Idea: 'R' = hold chin with hand as if thinking and say *R-R*

Bible Story

Read the Bible story from **one** of the following resources:

✔ Scripture: Matthew 3:13-17

✔ *A Child's First Bible* p. 152-153, 170-171

✔ *The New Bible in Pictures for Little Eyes* p. 252-253

Key Idea: Jesus was baptized.

Dramatic Play

Students stand in the center of the room with their eyes closed. You move to a new spot in the room and begin talking. Keeping their eyes closed, have students point in the direction of the talking. Next, without opening their eyes, have students follow your voice to where you are standing. Reverse roles. For a variation, tap instead of talking.

Key Idea: At Jesus' baptism, the people listened carefully to God's voice coming from heaven.

Letter Activity

Copy the *Hide and Seek 'R'* page. Have students circle, color, highlight, or point to the 'R's on the page. Younger students may need help in order to find any 'R's at all. It is not necessary to find all the 'R's. On the bottom of the page, have students connect 'R' to 'r' by tracing the dotted line from left to right.

Key Idea: Students should eventually recognize the capital and small letter 'R' within words.

Bible Activity

Copy the *BLUE is...* page. Have students find blue items in a magazine or a catalog to cut out. Use a marker to circle, box, or outline the blue items, so that students have a line to follow as they cut. Have students glue the items on the *BLUE is...* page. Save this page. A page will be added each week to make a color book.

Key Idea: Blue is for the river where John baptized Jesus. God's voice spoke from heaven telling everyone that Jesus is his Son.

Corresponding Music

The Singing Bible, Disc 4 – Track 2
Song Title: *"John the Baptist"*

Hide and Seek 'R'

Jesus our Lord is always right,

Always right,

Always right,

Jesus our Lord is always right,

He is the Son of God!

R _____ r

R _____ r

BLUE is...

**for the river
where John baptized Jesus.**

Jesus Grows Up and Begins His Ministry

Fingerplay

Do the fingerplay *"Jesus Is the Son of God"*. Focus on the sound and motion for the letter 'R'.

Key Idea: 'R' = hold chin with hand as if thinking and say *R-R*

Letter Activity

Use masking tape to make a large 'R' on the floor. Have students place blocks on the tape to trace the letter. Each time a block is placed on the tape, students make the letter **sound**.

Key Idea: Each letter has a name and a sound, just like animals do. For example, a lion may be named Leo, but it makes the sound, *Roar.*

Bible Story

Read the Bible story from **one** of the following resources:

✔ Scripture: Matthew 4:1-4, 7, 10

✔ *A Child's First Bible* p. 254-255

✔ *The New Bible in Pictures for Little Eyes* p. 254-255

Key Idea: Satan tested Jesus.

Bible Activity

Copy *Count on Me* (in Appendix). Direct students to draw symbols for 'no' by making 'X's' in the boxes. Younger students make 3 'X's' in each box. Older students make 4 'X's' in each box. Point to each 'X' as you count it with the students. Write the numbers on the lines below each box as you count. Say the numbers below the boxes to count by 3's or by 4's (counting either '3', '6', '9' ... or '4', '8', '12' ...).

Key Idea: Jesus said, *No,* to Satan 3 times.

Devotional Activity

Read and discuss the devotion from **one** of the following resources:

✔ *Big Thoughts for Little People*
Read the two pages for letter 'R'.

✔ *Teach Them to Your Children*
Read the two pages for letter 'R'.

✔ *My ABC Bible Verses*
Read the two pages for letter 'R'.

Key Idea: Share a devotional focusing on character traits or memory work based on the letter 'R'.

Corresponding Music

None this lesson

Jesus Grows Up and Begins His Ministry

Fingerplay

Do the fingerplay *"Jesus is the Son of God"*. Focus on the sound and motion for the letter 'R'.

Key Idea: 'R' = hold chin with hand as if thinking and say *R-R*

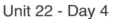

Letter Activity

Write a big 'R' on a piece of paper. Have students use fingerpaints, paints and paintbrushes, or playdough to fill in the letter.

Key Idea: Students will become familiar with the shape and appearance of the capital letter 'R'.

Bible Story

Read the Bible story from **one** of the following resources:

✔ Scripture: Mark 3:13-14
✔ *A Child's First Bible* p. 174-175
✔ *The New Bible in Pictures for Little Eyes* p. 256-257

Key Idea: Jesus chose disciples.

Bible Activity

Set out 12 stuffed animals or other props to represent the 12 disciples. Count the "disciples". Point to the stuffed animals one at a time, calling out the names of the 12 disciples. (Refer to Mark 3:16-19 for the names of the 12 disciples.)

Have students repeat each name. Then, have the students put the disciples in a line, so they are ready to follow Jesus.

Key Idea: Jesus called 12 disciples to follow him and learn from him during his time on earth.

Active Exploration

Remove the shade from a lamp. Darken the room, and plug in the lamp without its shade. (Make sure students do not touch the bulb on the lamp because it may be hot.) Have students take turns moving and making various shadows in the room. Experiment with ways to make larger shadows and smaller shadows.

Key Idea: Just like students' shadows follow them wherever they go, Jesus' disciples followed him wherever He went.

Corresponding Music

The Singing Bible, Disc 4 – Track 3
Song Titles: *"Twelve Guys"*

Jesus Grows Up and Begins His Ministry

Fingerplay

Do the fingerplay *"Jesus Is the Son of God"*. Focus on the sound and motion for the letter 'R'.

Key Idea: 'R' = hold chin with hand as if thinking and say *R-R*

Bible Story

Read the Bible story from **one** of the following resources:

✔ Scripture: John 2:2-3, 7-11

✔ *The New Bible in Pictures for Little Eyes* p. 258-259

Key Idea: Jesus made water into wine.

Math Activity

Write the number 6 on an index card or a piece of paper. Fill 6 cups or glasses with water to represent the jars of water in the story. Count each "jar" as it is set down. Ask students if we can turn the water in the jars into something else, like Jesus did. Have students explain why we can't do that. Write other numbers on cards and help students count out different objects one at a time to show those numbers.

Key Idea: Jesus did a miracle when He changed the water into wine.

Letter Activity

Use the 'R' flashcard from the Appendix. Have students trace the capital and small letter 'R's' on the flashcard with their fingers. Using the flashcard as a model, choose either sidewalk chalk or 2 crayons taped together and paper to write more 'R's'.

Key Idea: Practice the motions needed to make the letter 'R'.

Bible Activity

Fill 2 clear glasses with water. Add purple food coloring to one of the glasses. Ask students to guess what is in each glass. Have a student take a drink of the plain water and of the colored water. Explain that even though the two liquids looked different, they are the same thing. Ask students, *Did Jesus need to use tricks or magic to change the water to wine?*

Key Idea: Jesus could do miracles because He is God's Son. Miracles are not the same as magic.

Corresponding Music

The Singing Bible, Disc 4 – Track 4
Song Titles: *"Who Do You Say I Am?"*

Jesus' Miracles

Fingerplay

Do the fingerplay *"Jesus Did Miracles"*. Focus on the sound and motion for the letter 'S'.

Key Idea: 'S' = cover ears with hands, as if hearing a loud storm, and say *S-S*

Letter Activity

Copy the 'S' flashcard found in the Appendix. Show the letter side of the flashcard to the students. Read the Hint aloud. Demonstrate the motion and sound for 'S'. Have the students repeat it.

Key Idea: Students should eventually do the motion and say the sound for each flashcard without needing a *Hint* or a demonstration from you.

Bible Story

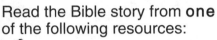

Read the Bible story from **one** of the following resources:

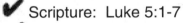 Scripture: Luke 5:1-7

 *A Child's First Bible* p. 178-179

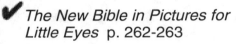 *The New Bible in Pictures for Little Eyes* p. 262-263

Key Idea: Peter caught so many fish.

Bible Activity

Copy the *ORANGE is...* page. Have students find orange items in a magazine or a catalog to cut out. Use a marker to circle, box, or outline the orange items, so that students have a line to follow as they cut. Have students glue the items on the *ORANGE is...* page. Save this page. A page will be added each week to make a color book.

Key Idea: Peter hadn't caught any fish all night. Orange is for all the fish that Peter and his friends caught after they did as Jesus said.

Math Activity

Stack paper and cut out a pile of simple paper fish or use goldfish crackers. Make 2 piles with different numbers of fish. Ask students, *Which pile has more fish?* Reinforce the answer by stating the number of fish in each pile and which is more. Continue with new piles. Extend the activity by asking which pile has less fish. Use piles of equal amounts to introduce the meaning of equal.

Key Idea: Jesus helped Peter catch more fish than Peter could count.

Corresponding Music

The Singing Bible, Disc 4 – Track 3
Song Title: *"Twelve Guys"*

Fingerplay: Jesus Did Miracles
(Sing to the tune of "*Row, Row, Row Your Boat*")

Days 1-5

Jesus did miracles.	*Cover mouth with hand, pull away*
People were surprised.	*Hands on cheeks*
No fish	*Shake head, "No"*
So many fish	*Open arms wide*
Wiggle! Wiggle!	*2 hands together, wiggle*
Squish!	*2 hands together, wiggle*

Jesus did miracles.	*Cover mouth with hand, pull away*
People were surprised.	*Hands on cheeks*
Storms blowing	*Cover ears*
Stop for him	*Face palm of hand out*
S...S...	*Cover ears*
They end.	*Pull hands off ears*

Jesus did miracles.	*Cover mouth with hand, pull away*
People were surprised.	*Hands on cheeks*
Sick ones,	*Hand on forehead*
Healed by him,	*Clap 2 times*
Cough never	*Cover mouth*
Again.	*Point to face and smile*

Jesus did miracles.	*Cover mouth with hand, pull away*
People were surprised.	*Hands on cheeks*
Dead ones	*Lay down*
Alive again	*Clap 2 times*
Tears turn into	*Trace tears on face with fingers*
Grins.	*Point to face and smile*

ORANGE is...

for all the fish
that Peter and his friends caught.

Jesus' Miracles

Fingerplay

Do the fingerplay *"Jesus Did Miracles"*. Focus on the sound and motion for the letter 'S'.

Key Idea: 'S' = cover ears with hands, as if hearing a loud storm, and say *S-S*

Bible Story

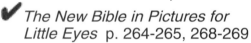

Read the Bible story from **one** of the following resources:

✔ Scripture: Luke 5:18-20, 24-26

✔ *A Child's First Bible* p. 180-181

✔ *The New Bible in Pictures for Little Eyes* p. 264-265, 268-269

Key Idea: Jesus healed the sick.

Devotional Activity

Read and discuss the devotion from **one** of the following resources:

✔ *Big Thoughts for Little People*
Read the two pages for letter 'S'.

✔ *Teach Them to Your Children*
Read the two pages for letter 'S'.

✔ *My ABC Bible Verses*
Read the two pages for letter 'S'.

Key Idea: Share a devotional focusing on character traits or memory work based on the letter 'S'.

Letter Activity

Copy the *Hide and Seek 'S'* page. Have students circle, color, highlight, or point to the 'S's' on the page. Younger students may need help in order to find any 'S's' at all. It is not necessary to find all the 'S's'. On the bottom of the page, have students connect 'S' to 's' by tracing the dotted line from left to right.

Key Idea: Students should eventually recognize the capital and small letter 'S' within words.

Bible Activity

Copy *Count on Me* (in Appendix). Direct students to draw band-aids by making pink, dotted rectangles in each of the boxes. Younger students make 3 band-aids in each box. Older students make 4 band-aids in each box. Point to each band-aid as you count it. Write the numbers on the lines below each box as you count. Say the numbers below the boxes to count by 3's or by 4's (counting either '3', '6', '9' ... or '4', '8', '12' ...).

Key Idea: Jesus took care of people's suffering and their "owies".

Corresponding Music

The Singing Bible, Disc 4 – Track 4
Song Title: *"Who Do You Say I Am?"*

Hide and Seek 'S'

Jesus did miracles.

People were surprised.

No fish

So many fish

Wiggle! Wiggle! Squish!

S _____ S

S _____ S

Jesus' Miracles

Fingerplay

Do the fingerplay *"Jesus Did Miracles"*. Focus on the sound and motion for the letter 'S'.

<u>Key Idea</u>: 'S' = cover ears with hands, as if hearing a loud storm, and say *S-S*

Letter Activity

Write a big 'S' on a piece of paper. Have students glue cotton balls or pieces of yarn to the letter. Younger students will need you to apply drops of glue on the letter for them first.

<u>Key Idea</u>: Students will become familiar with the shape and appearance of the capital letter 'S'.

Bible Story

Read the Bible story from **one** of the following resources:

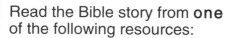

✔ Scripture: Luke 7:12-16

✔ *The New Bible in Pictures for Little Eyes* p. 274-275

<u>Key Idea</u>: Jesus raised a dead man.

Bible Activity

Discuss any people the students know that have died. Explain the following things to the students: Dead people cannot come to life again on earth. If those people who died believed in Jesus, they are in heaven right now. Someday we will see those people again in heaven, if we believe in Jesus too. The only reason Jesus could raise a man from the dead is because Jesus is God's Son.

<u>Key Idea</u>: Jesus could make a dead man live again on earth because Jesus is God's Son.

Active Exploration

Show students where their hearts are located. Ask students to sit quietly and feel their heartbeat. Have students jump up and down and then feel their heartbeat for any changes. Explain that the heartbeat is faster now because of the exercise that they did. Ask students, *Does your heart always pump this fast? Why, or why not?*

<u>Key Idea</u>: If our hearts stop beating for awhile, we die. Only Jesus could make a dead man live again.

Corresponding Music

The Singing Bible, Disc 4 – Track 4
Song Title: *"Who Do You Say I Am?"*

Jesus' Miracles

Fingerplay

Do the fingerplay *"Jesus Did Miracles"*. Focus on the sound and motion for the letter 'S'.

Key Idea: 'S' = cover ears with hands, as if hearing a loud storm, and say *S-S*

Letter Activity

Use masking tape to make a large 'S' on the floor. Have students drive a toy car or other toy vehicle on the tape to trace the letter. Have students say the letter **sound** as they drive.

Key Idea: Each letter has a name and a sound, just like animals do. For example, a cat may be named Fluffy, but it makes the sound, *Meow.*

Bible Story

Read the Bible story from **one** of the following resources:

✔ Scripture: Luke 8:23-25
✔ *A Child's First Bible* p. 192-193
✔ *The New Bible in Pictures for Little Eyes* p. 276-277

Key Idea: Jesus calmed the storm.

Bible Activity

Have students act out the storm in the story. Students hold their knees and rock like the boat, pound the floor with their fists like the waves, wave their arms in the air and blow like the wind, clap their hands like lightning, and stomp their feet like thunder. You pretend to be Jesus as you raise your hands and say, *Be still.* Have students stop and be silent. Ask students, *Can we do what Jesus did? Why, or why not?*

Key Idea: God created the wind and water, so they must obey him. Jesus is part of God.

Art Activity

Each student needs a **small, clear lidded container**. Give students the following directions: Tear off many bits of **blue and white paper** to be water, one chunk of **brown paper** for a boat, and **orange bits of paper** for fish. Place the paper in the container. Put the lid on. Shake the container to make a storm. Stop shaking and say, *Jesus stopped the storm.*

Key Idea: The wind and water obeyed Jesus. He is God's Son.

Corresponding Music

The Singing Bible, Disc 4 – Track 4
Song Title: *"Who Do You Say I Am?"*

Jesus' Miracles

Fingerplay

Do the fingerplay *"Jesus Did Miracles"*. Focus on the sound and motion for the letter 'S'.

<u>Key Idea</u>: 'S' = cover ears with hands, as if hearing a loud storm, and say *S-S*

Bible Story

Read the Bible story from **one** of the following resources:

 Scripture: Luke 8:41-42, 49-55

 *A Child's First Bible* p. 188-189

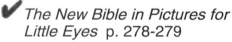 *The New Bible in Pictures for Little Eyes* p. 278-279

<u>Key Idea</u>: Jesus raised Jairus' daughter from the dead.

Dramatic Play

Spend time playing doctor to the students' stuffed animals, dolls, or toy figures. Use blankets, adhesive bandages, paper towels for casts, craft sticks with red lines drawn on them as thermometers, paper for notes, file folders for charts, and other play medical instruments.

<u>Key Idea</u>: The doctors could not make the little girl well, so she died. But, Jesus could heal her and raise her from the dead.

Letter Activity

Use the 'S' flashcard from the Appendix. Have students trace the capital and small letter 'S' on the flashcard with their fingers. Using the flashcard as a model, give students either a small amount of cooking oil or liquid soap on an aluminum pan or plate to use to write more 'S's'.

<u>Key Idea</u>: Practice the motions needed to make the letter 'S'.

Bible Activity

Have students lay a stuffed animal on the floor to be the little girl who died. Cover the "girl" up with a blanket and weep over her. You pretend to be Jesus, take the little girl's hand, and tell her to get up.

Have the students make the stuffed animal stand up and pretend to give it something to eat. Ask students to clap in amazement.

<u>Key Idea</u>: Jesus could do miracles, because He's God's Son.

Corresponding Music

The Singing Bible, Disc 4 – Track 4
Song Title: *"Who Do You Say I Am?"*

More of Jesus' Miracles

Fingerplay

Do the fingerplay *"Time to Move"*. Focus on the sound and motion for the letter 'T'.

Key Idea: 'T' = tap wrist with finger several times and say *T-T*

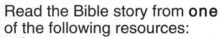

Bible Story

Read the Bible story from **one** of the following resources:

✔ Scripture: Mark 8:22-25
✔ *A Child's First Bible* p. 190-191
✔ *The New Bible in Pictures for Little Eyes* p. 280-281

Key Idea: Jesus healed the blind.

Active Exploration

Place a variety of items in a sack or a pillowcase. Possible ideas for items include a block, a spoon, a ball, a toy car, a sock, a clothespin, a cottonball, and a baby bottle. Have students take turns reaching and feeling one of the items, guessing what it is, and pulling it out to check. When all of the items have been pulled out, change the game. Instead tell students which item to find by feeling in the bag.

Key Idea: A blind person often feels to discover what something is.

Letter Activity

Copy the 'T' flashcard found in the Appendix. Show the letter side of the flashcard to the students. Read the *Hint* aloud. Demonstrate the motion and sound for 'T'. Have the students repeat it.

Key Idea: Students should eventually do the motion and say the sound for each flashcard without needing a *Hint* or a demonstration.

Bible Activity

Copy *Count on Me* (in Appendix). Direct students to draw eyes by making brown circles with a dot in each center in the boxes. Younger students make 3 eyes in each box. Older students make 4 eyes in each box. Point to each eye as you count it. Write the numbers on the lines below each box as you count. Say the numbers below the boxes to count by 3's or by 4's (counting either '3', '6', '9' ... or '4', '8', '12' ...).

Key Idea: Jesus healed the blind and did many other miracles to show He is God's Son.

Corresponding Music

The Singing Bible, Disc 4 – Track 4
Song Title: *"Who Do You Say I Am?"*

Fingerplay: Time to Move

Days 1-5

Stomp your feet.	*Stomp your feet*
Clap your hands.	*Clap your hands*
Jesus healed both girls and boys.	*Point up*
Stomp your feet.	*Stomp your feet*
Clap your hands.	*Clap your hands*
T-Time to jump for joy.	*Tap wrist with finger, jump up*
March in place.	*March in place*
Touch the ground.	*Touch the ground*
Jesus walked out to the boat.	*Point up*
March in place.	*March in place*
Touch the ground.	*Touch the ground*
T-Time to spin and float.	*Tap wrist with finger, spin, tiptoe*
Touch your toes.	*Touch your toes*
Twist and turn.	*Twist your body, spin around*
Jesus made a man alive.	*Point up*
Touch your toes.	*Touch your toes*
Twist and turn.	*Twist your body, spin around*
Time to praise, God on high.	*Tap wrist with finger, reach up*

More of Jesus' Miracles

Fingerplay

Do the fingerplay *"Time to Move"*. Focus on the sound and motion for the letter 'T'.

<u>Key Idea</u>: 'T' = tap wrist with finger several times and say *T-T*

Bible Story

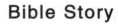

Read the Bible story from **one** of the following resources:

 Scripture: Luke 9:12-17

 *A Child's First Bible* p. 198-199

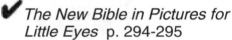 *The New Bible in Pictures for Little Eyes* p. 294-295

<u>Key Idea</u>: Jesus fed thousands.

Math Activity

Place a strip of masking tape vertically on the table. Tear a slice of bread into 5 pieces and place them on one side of the tape. Count the pieces. Move several pieces over to the other side of the tape. Count again. Show that no matter how we move the pieces there are always 5. For older students, write a number sentence each time you show a different way to make 5.

<u>Key Idea</u>: Jesus made bread from 5 loaves to feed thousands of people. Can we do that? Why not?

Letter Activity

Copy the *Hide and Seek 'T'* page. Have students circle, color, highlight, or point to the 'T's' on the page. Younger students may need help in order to find any 'T's' at all. It is not necessary to find all the 'T's'. On the bottom of the page, have students connect 'T' to 't' by tracing the dotted line from left to right.

<u>Key Idea</u>: Students should eventually recognize the capital and small letter 'T' within words.

Bible Activity

Copy the *BROWN is...* page. Have students find brown items in a magazine or a catalog to cut out. Use a marker to circle, box, or outline the brown items, so that students have a line to follow as they cut. Have students glue the items on the *BROWN is...* page. Save this page. A page will be added each week to make a color book.

<u>Key Idea</u>: Brown is for the bread that Jesus used to feed thousands of people on the hillside.

Corresponding Music

The Singing Bible, Disc 4 – Track 4
Song Title: *"Who Do You Say I Am?"*

Hide and Seek 'T'

Jesus made a man alive.

Touch your toes.

Twist and turn.

Time to praise, God on high.

T ----------------------------------- t

T ----------------------------------- t

BROWN is...

for the bread that Jesus
used to feed thousands of people.

More of Jesus' Miracles

Fingerplay

Do the fingerplay *"Time to Move"*. Focus on the sound and motion for the letter 'T'.

<u>Key Idea</u>: 'T' = tap wrist with finger several times and say *T-T*

Bible Story

Read the Bible story from **one** of the following resources:

✔ Scripture: Mark 6:47-51

✔ *A Child's First Bible* p. 194-195

✔ *The New Bible in Pictures for Little Eyes* p. 296-297

<u>Key Idea</u>: Jesus walked on water.

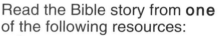

Art Activity

Have students **fingerpaint white** waves on **blue paper**. Sprinkle **salt** on the wet paint. After the paint dries, cut a horizontal slit in the paper and tape the edges of the slit. On each student's index finger, draw eyes, mouth, and hair to be Jesus. Have students slide Jesus through the slit and show him walking on the water. Older students may add a boat and make a cutout of Jesus to glue on a craft stick instead.

<u>Key Idea</u>: Jesus was able to walk on the water because He created it.

Letter Activity

Use masking tape to make a large 'T' on the floor. Have students tiptoe on the tape to trace the letter. Then, have students jump off the end of the letter saying the letter **sound** as they jump.

<u>Key Idea</u>: Each letter has a name and a sound, just like animals do. For example, a dog may be named Rover, but it makes the sound, *Ruff.*

Bible Activity

Fill part of a sink or small tub with water. Put towels on the floor around the sink or tub. Place an object that floats in the water to represent the boat in the story. Add a few drops of dish soap to make waves. Have students gently splash the water and let the boat begin to sink. Use an object to represent Jesus walking on the water toward the boat. As Jesus gets in the boat, ask students to stop splashing.

<u>Key Idea</u>: We need to trust Jesus. He created all things, even us.

Corresponding Music

The Singing Bible, Disc 4 – Track 4
Song Title: *"Who Do You Say I Am?"*

More of Jesus' Miracles

Fingerplay

Do the fingerplay *"Time to Move"*. Focus on the sound and motion for the letter 'T'.

<u>Key Idea</u>: 'T' = tap wrist with finger several times and say *T-T*

Letter Activity

Write a big 'T' on a piece of paper. Have students glue dried macaroni or raisins to the letter. Younger students will need you to apply drops of glue on the letter for them first.

<u>Key Idea</u>: Students will become familiar with the shape and appearance of the capital letter 'T'.

Bible Story

Read the Bible story from **one** of the following resources:

✔ Scripture: John 11:17, 38, 41-44
✔ *A Child's First Bible* p. 210-211
✔ *The New Bible in Pictures for Little Eyes* p. 300-301

<u>Key Idea</u>: Lazarus lived again.

Bible Activity

Even though Lazarus loved Jesus and was his friend, Lazarus got sick and died. Ask students, *If we love Jesus, does that mean that nothing bad will ever happen to us?*

Point out that because there is sin in the world, bad things happen. But, Jesus is always with us, even when bad things happen. We can always talk to him, and He will hear us. Someday we will be in heaven with him and all the bad things will pass away.

<u>Key Idea</u>: Jesus has power over life and death. Those who believe in him will live in heaven someday.

Dramatic Play

Guide students through the following steps: Make a cave by rolling playdough into a ball and hollowing out a hole in it. Make a stone by flattening playdough. Cut thin paper towel strips to wrap around a craft stick or other small toy person to represent Lazarus. Place Lazarus in the cave. Put the stone over the mouth of the cave. Roll the stone away. Unwrap the figure. Say, *Jesus made me alive again!*

<u>Key Idea</u>: Jesus brought Lazarus back to life again.

Corresponding Music

The Singing Bible, Disc 4 – Track 4
Song Title: *"Who Do You Say I Am?"*

More of Jesus' Miracles

Fingerplay

Do the fingerplay *"Time to Move"*. Focus on the sound and motion for the letter 'T'.

<u>Key Idea</u>: 'T' = tap wrist with finger several times and say *T-T*

Bible Story

Read the Bible story from **one** of the following resources:

✔ Scripture: Luke 17:12-19

✔ *A Child's First Bible* p. 212-213

✔ *The New Bible in Pictures for Little Eyes* p. 314-315

<u>Key Idea</u>: One man thanked Jesus.

Devotional Activity

Read and discuss the devotion from **one** of the following resources:

✔ *Big Thoughts for Little People*
Read the two pages for letter 'T'.

✔ *Teach Them to Your Children*
Read the two pages for letter 'T'.

✔ *My ABC Bible Verses*
Read the two pages for letter 'T'.

<u>Key Idea</u>: Share a devotional focusing on character traits or memory work based on the letter 'T'.

Letter Activity

Use the 'T' flashcard from the Appendix. Have students trace the capital and small letter 'T' on the flashcard with their fingers. Using the flashcard as a model, choose either pudding, chocolate syrup, baby food, or fingerpaint on a plate, pan, or piece of paper for students to write more 'T's'.

<u>Key Idea</u>: Practice the motions needed to make the letter 'T'.

Bible Activity

Take turns giving students a compliment and having them respond, *Thank you*. Ask students, *Why was Jesus sad when only 1 of the 10 men He healed said, "Thank you"? How does Jesus feel when we forget to tell him thank you? What are some things we should thank Jesus for?* Say a prayer of thanks that includes the things the students listed.

<u>Key Idea</u>: We need to remember to thank Jesus for the good things He does for us.

Corresponding Music

The Singing Bible, Disc 4 – Track 4
Song Title: *"Who Do You Say I Am?"*

Jesus' Parables

Fingerplay

Do the fingerplay *"What Do You Know?"* Focus on reviewing the sounds and motions for the letters.

<u>Key Idea</u>: Practice the sounds and motions for the letters 'A-T'.

Bible Story

Read the Bible story from **one** of the following resources:

✔ Scripture: Matthew 7:24-27

✔ *The New Bible in Pictures for Little Eyes* p. 272-273

<u>Key Idea</u>: The wise man built his house on the rock.

Art Activity

Give each student a piece of **grey** or **brown construction paper**. Have students draw rocks all over their papers. Cut many **different sized strips of paper** for students to use to build "houses" that stand up. The papers with the rocks drawn on them will be foundations. Students may cut, tear, fold, and **tape** the paper strips any way they choose to make their houses.

<u>Key Idea</u>: The wise man built his house on the rocks. We should be wise and build our life on Jesus, our rock.

Letter Activity

This is a review week. Review all the flashcards from the previous weeks. Show the letter side of each flashcard to the students. Have them respond with the motion and sound. If needed, read the *Hint* or demonstrate the motion and sound.

<u>Key Idea</u>: Students should eventually do the motion and say the sound for each flashcard without needing a *Hint* or a demonstration from you.

Bible Activity

Have students use blocks to build 2 quick "houses". One house should be built on a strong, level base, like the floor. The other house should be built on an uneven surface, like a crumpled up towel. After the houses are built, have students pretend to be rain coming down and pulling the towel out from under the house, so it tumbles. Leave the house on the strong base standing.

<u>Key Idea</u>: Jesus is our strength, like the rocks. We need to follow him to stay standing strong.

Corresponding Music

None this lesson

Fingerplay: What Do You Know?

Days 1-5

We've learned about *A-A-Adam*	*Hands on cheeks in surprise*
And *B-B-Boat,*	*Hug yourself and rock side-to-side*
C-C-Clippity clop	*Tap palms on thighs in rhythm*
And *D-D-Dusty* camel.	*Hold reins of camel and move up-down-up-down*
E-E-Empty jars	*Shake hand to shake empty jar*
And *F-F-Fire,*	*Wiggle 10 fingers like flames*
G-G-Gurgle	*Hold nose, put hand up*
And *H-H-Helping* hands.	*Lace fingers, move up and down*
I-Impossible	*Push palms up as if lifting*
And *J-J-Joyful* jumping,	*2 fingers jump on palm of hand*
K-K-clapping hands	*Clap hands above head*
And *L-L-La-La-La.*	*Swing hand back and forth*
M-M-Miracles	*Pat hand over mouth, pull it away*
And *N-N-Naughty* king,	*Tap top of hand with 2 fingers*
O-O-Off	*Brush one hand with the other*
And *P-P-Pulling* oars.	*Make fists and pull them in*
Q-Q-Quivering	*Shake whole body*
And *R-R-Ready* to choose,	*Hold chin with hand, thinking*
S-S-Storms blowing	*Cover ears*
And *T-Time* to move.	*Tap wrist with finger, jump up*

Fingerplay: What Do You Know?
(continued)

Now, as Jesus	*Point up*
Tells parables,	*Cup hands around mouth*
He shares lessons	*Point up*
That we need to know.	*Point to head*
Just like the others	*Open palms together like Bible*
God has plans for you too.	*Point up, then point to yourself*
Never forget	*Shake head, "No"*
What God can do!	*Spread arms wide*

Jesus' Parables

Fingerplay

Do the fingerplay *"What Do You Know?"* Focus on reviewing the sounds and motions for the letters.

Key Idea: Practice the sounds and motions for the letters 'A-T'.

Bible Story

Read the Bible story from **one** of the following resources:

✔ Scripture: Luke 10:30-37

✔ *A Child's First Bible* p. 204-205

✔ *The New Bible in Pictures for Little Eyes* p. 282-283

Key Idea: The good neighbor helps.

Dramatic Play

On the floor, make a path using two parallel masking tape lines several feet apart. Lay a stuffed toy or other prop beside the path to be the hurt man. Younger students sit on a pillow, hold onto its edges, and scoot down the path. Older students roll a ball slowly down the path guiding it with their feet. All students go down the path twice, ignoring the hurt man. On the third trip down the path, students stop, help the man, and take him along.

Key Idea: We should help others.

Letter Activity

Choose one letter from 'A-T' to review. Write that letter on a big piece of paper. Use water to thin glue and have students "paint" the glue on the letter. Then, sprinkle either salt, coffee grounds, glitter, or any kind of spice on the glue. Younger students will need you to help them with the sprinkling part.

Key Idea: Students will become familiar with the shape and appearance of the capital letters.

Bible Activity

Point out that sometimes we ignore people that need help. Some examples include the following: hearing someone crying but not comforting them, watching someone clear the table after a meal instead of helping, not listening to someone the first time they tell you to do a chore, seeing toys to pick up but playing instead, and not playing with a little brother or sister when they want to play with you.

Key Idea: Jesus says we should help others, just like the Samaritan in the story.

Corresponding Music

The Singing Bible, Disc 4 – Track 5
Song Title: *"Blessed Are..."*

Jesus' Parables

Fingerplay

Do the fingerplay *"What Do You Know?"* Focus on reviewing the sounds and motions for the letters.

<u>Key Idea</u>: Practice the sounds and motions for the letters 'A-T'.

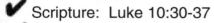

Bible Story

Reread the Bible story from day 2 in **one** of the following resources:

✔ Scripture: Luke 10:30-37

✔ *A Child's First Bible* p.204-205

✔ *The New Bible in Pictures for Little Eyes* p. 282-283

<u>Key Idea</u>: The good neighbor loves.

Devotional Activity

Read and discuss the devotion from **one** of the following resources:

✔ *Big Thoughts for Little People*
Review verses for 'Q', 'R', 'S', 'T'

✔ *Teach Them to Your Children*
Review verses for 'Q', 'R', 'S', 'T'

✔ *My ABC Bible Verses*
Review verses for 'Q', 'R', 'S', 'T'

<u>Key Idea</u>: Share a devotional focusing on character traits or memory work based on the letters 'Q', 'R', 'S', 'T'.

Letter Activity

Choose one or more of the letters 'A-T' to review. Use masking tape to make the large review letter on the floor. Have students sit on a pillow and scoot on the tape to trace the letter. Have students say the letter **sound** as they scoot.

<u>Key Idea</u>: Each letter has a name and a sound, just like animals do. For example, a horse may be named Silver, but it makes the sound, *Neigh.*

Bible Activity

Copy the *RED is...* page. Have students find red items in a magazine or a catalog to cut out. Use a marker to circle, box, or outline the red items, so that students have a line to follow as they cut. Have students glue the items on the *RED is...* page. Save this page. A page will be added each week to make a color book.

<u>Key Idea</u>: Red is for the Red Cross, which is a symbol for helping others. Jesus asks us to be kind and helpful to others.

Corresponding Music

The Singing Bible, Disc 4 – Track 5
Song Title: *"Blessed Are..."*

RED is...

for the Red Cross,
which is a symbol for helping others.

Hide and Seek Review

We've learned about Q-Q-Quivering,

And R-R-Ready to choose,

S-S-Storms blowing,

And T-T-Time to move.

Q

R

S

T

t

q

s

r

Jesus' Parables

Fingerplay

Do the fingerplay *"What Do You Know?"* Focus on reviewing the sounds and motions for the letters.

<u>Key Idea</u>: Practice the sounds and motions for the letters 'A-T'.

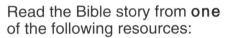

Bible Story

Read the Bible story from **one** of the following resources:

 Scripture: Luke 12:16-21

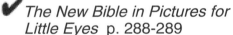 *The New Bible in Pictures for Little Eyes* p. 288-289

<u>Key Idea</u>: The rich man didn't love God.

Math Activity

Outline the shape of a small barn on the floor with masking tape. Have students use playing cards, blocks, or toy cars placed side to side to fill in the area. Outline a bigger barn with masking tape. Have students use the same kind of objects to fill in this area. Count and compare the number of items it took to cover the two barns. For older students, write a number sentence using the greater than symbol to compare the 2 areas.

<u>Key Idea</u>: We should not be greedy. God says to think of others.

Letter Activity

Copy the *Hide-n-Seek Review* page. Choose a letter from 'Q-T' to review. Have students circle, color, highlight, or point to the chosen letter. Younger students may need help in order to find any of the chosen letters. On the bottom of the page, have students draw a line to connect each capital letter to its matching lowercase letter.

<u>Key Idea</u>: Students should eventually recognize the capital and small letters 'Q-T' within words.

Bible Activity

Copy *Count on Me* (in Appendix). Direct students to draw coins by making gray colored circles with cent signs on them in each of the boxes. Younger students make 3 coins in each box. Older students make 4 coins in each box. Point to each coin as you count it with the students. Write the numbers on the lines below each box as you count. Say the numbers below the boxes to count by 3's or 4's (counting either '3', '6', '9' ... or '4', '8', '12' ...).

<u>Key Idea</u>: God owns what we have.

Corresponding Music

The Singing Bible, Disc 4 – Track 5 Song Title: *"Blessed Are..."*

Jesus' Parables

Fingerplay

Do the fingerplay *"What Do You Know?"* Focus on reviewing the sounds and motions for the letters.

<u>Key Idea</u>: Practice the sounds and motions for the letters 'A-T'.

Letter Activity

Choose one or more of the flashcards from the previous weeks to review. Have students trace the capital and small letters on the flashcards with their fingers. Using the flashcards as models, choose either markers and markerboards or pieces of carpet and fingers to practice writing more letters.

<u>Key Idea</u>: Practice the motions needed to make the letters.

Bible Story

Read the Bible story from **one** of the following resources:

✔ Scripture: Luke 8:4-8

✔ *The New Bible in Pictures for Little Eyes* p. 292-293

<u>Key Idea</u>: The farmer sowed his seeds.

Bible Activity

Talk about how Christians can help God's Word grow in others, like a seed growing in good soil. We can teach others songs about the Lord, study the Bible with others, teach others to pray, take others to church, teach others to treat their body as God's temple, and teach others his commands.

<u>Key Idea</u>: We must spread the seed, God's Word, even though it doesn't <u>always</u> grow.

Active Exploration

Have students test whether objects glide or drop to the floor when they are tossed into the air. Possible objects to test include the following: tissue, lightweight block, cotton ball, coin, piece of paper, piece of yarn, eraser, and a stuffed toy. After tossing each object into the air, students place it into a pile for those that glide or a pile for those that drop. Ask students, *Would seeds glide or drop?*

<u>Key Idea</u>: The farmer's seeds glided and landed different places.

Corresponding Music

None this lesson

More of Jesus' Parables

Fingerplay

Do the fingerplay *"The Stories Jesus Told"*. Focus on the sound and motion for the letter 'U'.

Key Idea: 'U' = shake head 'no' and say *U-U*

Bible Story

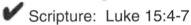

Read the Bible story from **one** of the following resources:

✔ Scripture: Luke 15:4-7

✔ *A Child's First Bible* p. 208-209

✔ *The New Bible in Pictures for Little Eyes* p. 306-307

Key Idea: The lost sheep need God.

Dramatic Play

Use cotton balls to be sheep. Count and hide the "sheep" around the room. Students are shepherds that search for the sheep. A laundry basket or other container is the sheep pen. Each time a sheep is found, students carry it carefully back to the pen. Older students place the sheep on a spoon to carry it back to the pen. Count to make sure all of the sheep have returned to the pen.

Key Idea: God is our shepherd, and we are his sheep.

Letter Activity

Copy the 'U' flashcard found in the Appendix. Show the letter side of the flashcard to the students. Read the *Hint* aloud. Demonstrate the motion and sound for 'U'. Have the students repeat it.

Key Idea: Students should eventually do the motion and say the sound for each flashcard without needing a *Hint* or a demonstration from you.

Bible Activity

Copy *Count on Me* (in Appendix). Direct students to draw shepherds' staffs by making brown hooks in the boxes. Younger students make 3 staffs in each box. Older students make 4 staffs in each box. Point to each staff as you count it with the students. Write the numbers on the lines below each box as you count. Say the numbers below the boxes to count by 3's or by 4's (counting either '3', '6', '9' ... or '4', '8', '12' ...).

Key Idea: God watches over us just like a shepherd watches over his sheep. God knows each one of us.

Corresponding Music

The Singing Bible, Disc 4 – Track 12
Song Title: *"Love, Love"*

Fingerplay: The Stories Jesus Told

Learn from stories Jesus told.	*Hold palms open like a book*
Tiptoe, tiptoe on your toes.	*Tiptoe around on toes*
Stop and freeze where you're at.	*Strike a frozen pose*
Answer this question I will ask...	*Point to mind*
Does the shepherd leave his sheep?	*Hold hands out*
U...U... No!	*Shake head, "No"*
Close watch he keeps.	*Shade eyes with hand*
Learn from stories Jesus told.	*Hold palms open like a book*
Tiptoe, tiptoe on your toes.	*Tiptoe around on toes*
Stop and freeze where you're at.	*Strike a frozen pose*
Answer this question I will ask...	*Point to mind*
Is the father mad at his son?	*Hold hands out*
U...U... No!	*Shake head, "No"*
Forgiving, shows his love.	*Cross arms on chest*
Learn from stories Jesus told.	*Hold palms open like a book*
Tiptoe, tiptoe on your toes.	*Tiptoe around on toes*
Stop and freeze where you're at.	*Strike a frozen pose*
Answer this question I will ask...	*Point to mind*
Is money ours alone?	*Hold hands out*
U...U... No!	*Shake head, "No"*
It's God's to own.	*Point up*

More of Jesus' Parables

Fingerplay

Do the fingerplay *"The Stories Jesus Told"*. Focus on the sound and motion for the letter 'U'.

Key Idea: 'U' = shake head 'no' and say *U-U*

Bible Story

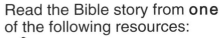

Read the Bible story from **one** of the following resources:

✔ Scripture: Luke 15:11-19
✔ *A Child's First Bible* p. 214-215
✔ *The New Bible in Pictures for Little Eyes* p. 310-311

Key Idea: One son left home.

Math Activity

Trace each student's feet on paper and cut them out. Show students how to use their paper feet to measure distances by placing the feet heel-to-toe. Move one paper foot at a time and count the feet as you measure. Direct students to measure the distance to a certain object or the distance between two objects. Have older students compare the distances and show them that 12 inches equals one foot.

Key Idea: The son left his father and walked off to see distant places.

Letter Activity

Write a big 'U' on a piece of paper. Have students glue dry 'O'-shaped cereal or dried beans to the letter. Younger students will need you to apply drops of glue on the letter for them first.

Key Idea: Students will become familiar with the shape and appearance of the capital letter 'U'.

Bible Activity

Act out the Bible story. You be the father and have students be the young son. Pretend to hand your son money. Give students the following directions: *Take the money and put it in your bag. Pretend to pick up your bags, turn to wave good-bye, and skip off down the road.* You shake your head sadly as you watch your son go.

Key Idea: The young son did not want to listen to his father. He wanted to do things his own way.

Corresponding Music

The Singing Bible, Disc 4 – Track 12
Song Title: *"Love, Love"*

More of Jesus' Parables

Fingerplay

Do the fingerplay *"The Stories Jesus Told"*. Focus on the sound and motion for the letter 'U'.

<u>Key Idea</u>: 'U' = shake head 'no' and say *U-U*

Bible Story

Read the Bible story from **one** of the following resources:

✔ Scripture: Luke 15:20-24

✔ *A Child's First Bible* p. 214-215

✔ *The New Bible in Pictures for Little Eyes* p. 312-313

<u>Key Idea</u>: The son came home.

Art Activity

Cut a rectangular shape out of a **file folder** or other piece of **tagboard** to be a path. Have students use the **hole punch** to punch holes around the edge of the path. The holes are the steps the son walked as he left home and came back again. Students may **color** or **fingerpaint** rocks on the path. Older students may use **yarn** with the tip taped to lace in and out of the holes.

<u>Key Idea</u>: God is like the father in the story, waiting to welcome us back after we have sinned.

Letter Activity

Use masking tape to make a large 'U' on the floor. Have students walk a stuffed animal on the tape to trace the letter. Then, have students walk the letter themselves, saying the letter **sound** as they walk.

<u>Key Idea</u>: Each letter has a name and a sound, just like animals do.
For example, a cow may be named Bessie, but it makes the sound, *Moo.*

Bible Activity

Have students practice forgiving someone that has upset them. Have stuffed animals be the people needing forgiveness. Some role plays for students to do include someone spilling something of theirs, knocking over their toy tower, tripping them, saying, *I don't like you,* pointing and laughing at them, and running into them. Each time, have the "offender" say that he is sorry. Then, the "offended" person needs to say, *I forgive you.* Switch roles if time allows.

<u>Key Idea</u>: The father forgave his son and welcomed him back home.

Corresponding Music

The Singing Bible, Disc 4 – Track 12
Song Title: *"Love, Love"*

More of Jesus' Parables

Fingerplay

Do the fingerplay *"The Stories Jesus Told"*. Focus on the sound and motion for the letter 'U'.

<u>Key Idea</u>: 'U' = shake head 'no' and say *U-U*

Bible Story

Read the Bible story from **one** of the following resources:

 Scripture: Luke 20:9-16

✔ *The New Bible in Pictures for Little Eyes* p. 316-317

<u>Key Idea</u>: The grape growers sinned.

Active Exploration

Say to students, *Just like the father in the story noticed that his son was missing, we need to see what is missing too.* Set out several objects in front of the students. Have the students close their eyes as you remove one of the objects and hide it behind your back. The students need to name the object that is missing. Later, give students a chance to remove one object while you have your eyes closed.

<u>Key Idea</u>: Sin can't be hidden from God. God gives us many chances to turn from our sin.

Letter Activity

Copy the *Hide and Seek 'U'* page. Have students circle, color, highlight, or point to the 'U's on the page. Younger students may need help in order to find any 'U's at all. It is not necessary to find all the 'U's. On the bottom of the page, have students connect 'U' to 'u' by tracing the dotted line from left to right.

<u>Key Idea</u>: Students should eventually recognize the capital and small letter 'U' within words.

Bible Activity

Copy the *PURPLE is...* page. Have students find purple items in a magazine or a catalog to cut out. Use a marker to circle, box, or outline the purple items, so that students have a line to follow as they cut. Have students glue the items on the *PURPLE is...* page. Save this page. A page will be added each week to make a color book.

<u>Key Idea</u>: Purple is for the grapes in the parable. All that we have belongs to the Lord.

Corresponding Music

None this lesson

Hide and Seek 'U'

Answer this question I will ask...

Is money ours alone?

U... U... No!

It's God's to own.

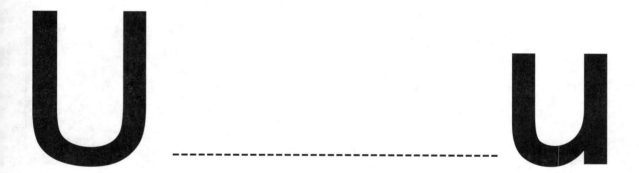

PURPLE is...

for the grapes in the parable.

More of Jesus' Parables

Fingerplay

Do the fingerplay *"The Stories Jesus Told"*. Focus on the sound and motion for the letter 'U'.

<u>Key Idea</u>: 'U' = shake head, *No,* and say *U-U*

Bible Story

Read the Bible story from **one** of the following resources:

✔ Scripture: Matthew 22:2-3, 8-10

✔ *The New Bible in Pictures for Little Eyes* p. 324-325

<u>Key Idea</u>: The dinner guests were invited.

Devotional Activity

Read and discuss the devotion from **one** of the following resources:

✔ *Big Thoughts for Little People*
Read the two pages for letter 'U'.

✔ *Teach Them to Your Children*
Read the two pages for letter 'U'.

✔ *My ABC Bible Verses*
Read the two pages for letter 'U'.

<u>Key Idea</u>: Share a devotional focusing on character traits or memory work based on the letter 'U'.

Letter Activity

Use the 'U' flashcard from the Appendix. Have students trace the capital and small letter 'U's" on the flashcard with their fingers. Using the flashcard as a model, choose either a bar of soap on a mirror or an ice cube on construction paper to write more 'U's'.

<u>Key Idea</u>: Practice the motions needed to make the letter 'U'.

Bible Activity

Give students the following directions: *Help prepare for a pretend banquet by setting out play food and plates. Scatter stuffed toys or other figures on the floor away from the banquet area. Pretend to open the doors wide and hold out your arms to welcome the guests. Look around to see that no one has come. Go out and gather the stuffed toys or other figures and bring them to the banquet.*

<u>Key Idea</u>: Just as the man invited his friends to the banquet, Jesus invites us to heaven. Will you accept his invitation?

Corresponding Music

The Singing Bible, Disc 4 – Track 12
Song Title: *"Love, Love"*

Jesus' Teachings

Fingerplay

Do the fingerplay *"If You Believe in Jesus"*. Focus on the sound and motion for the letter 'V'.

Key Idea: 'V' = put your hand on your voice box, feel the vibration in your throat, and say *V-V*

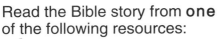

Bible Story

Read the Bible story from **one** of the following resources:

 Scripture: John 2:13-16

 The New Bible in Pictures for Little Eyes p. 260-261

Key Idea: Jesus cleared the temple.

Dramatic Play

Set out chairs and a Bible to be the church. Have students practice showing respect in "God's house" by doing the following actions: walk calmly, sit quietly, speak in a soft voice, pray with eyes closed and hands still, greet others with a handshake, handle the Bible with care, and sing along with the song *"Jesus Loves the Little Children"*.

Key Idea: Point out that God's house is special, and we need to show him that we love him when we are in his house.

Letter Activity

Copy the 'V' flashcard found in the Appendix. Show the letter side of the flashcard to the students. Read the *Hint* aloud. Demonstrate the motion and sound for 'V'. Have the students repeat it.

Key Idea: Students should eventually do the motion and say the sound for each flashcard without needing a *Hint* or a demonstration from you.

Bible Activity

Copy the *BLACK is...* page. Have students find black items in a magazine or a catalog to cut out. Use a marker to circle, box, or outline the black items, so that students have a line to follow as they cut.

Have students glue the items on the *BLACK is...* page. Save this page. A page will be added each week to make a color book.

Key Idea: Black is for anger. Jesus was upset when he cleared the men out of the temple for buying and selling things in God's house.

Corresponding Music

None this lesson

Fingerplay: If You Believe in Jesus
(Sing to the tune of *"If You're Happy and You Know It"*)

If you believe in Jesus	*Point to heart*
Spin around.	*Spin around*
If you believe in Jesus	*Point to heart*
Spin around.	*Spin around*
If you believe in Jesus	*Point to heart*
And you really try to please him,	*Point to face and smile*
If you believe in Jesus	*Point to heart*
Spin around.	*Spin around*

If Jesus hears your voice	*Touch throat with hand*
Get on your knees.	*Kneel down*
If Jesus hears your voice	*Touch throat with hand*
Get on your knees.	*Kneel down*
If Jesus hears your *v-v-voice*	*Touch throat with hand*
And you pray before each choice,	*Fold hands to pray*
If Jesus hears your voice	*Touch throat with hand*
Get on your knees.	*Kneel down*

If God cares for you	*Cross arms on chest*
Jump up high.	*Jump high*
If God cares for you	*Cross arms on chest*
Jump up high.	*Jump high*
If God cares for you	*Cross arms on chest*
And you really want him to,	*Point to head*
If God cares for you	*Cross arms on chest*
Jump up high.	*Jump high*

BLACK is...

for anger toward the men
that were buying and selling in God's house.

Jesus' Teachings

Fingerplay

Do the fingerplay *"If You Believe in Jesus"*. Focus on the sound and motion for the letter 'V'.

<u>Key Idea</u>: 'V' = put your hand on your voice box, feel the vibration in your throat, and say *V-V*

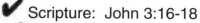

Bible Story

Read the Bible story from **one** of the following resources:

✔ Scripture: John 3:16-18

✔ *A Child's First Bible* p. 172-173, 184-185

✔ *The New Bible in Pictures for Little Eyes* p. 266-267, 270-271

<u>Key Idea</u>: Believe in Jesus.

Math Activity

Stack papers to cut out at least 10 hearts. Draw a cross on one side of each heart. Get 2 index cards. Label 1 card with a cloud to show heaven. Label the other card with a fire to show hell. Shake the hearts and drop them on the table. Under the cloud, line up any hearts with the cross side showing. Under the fire, line up any hearts with the blank side showing. Count each set.

<u>Key Idea</u>: We must have Jesus in our hearts to go to heaven.

Letter Activity

Write a big 'V' on a piece of paper. Have students use fingerpaints, paints and paintbrushes, or playdough to fill in the letter.

<u>Key Idea</u>: Students will become familiar with the shape and appearance of the capital letter 'V'.

Bible Activity

Discuss some of the following questions with the students: How do we get to heaven? What does Jesus want us to do? How can we have Jesus be our friend? What does Jesus do for us? (Possible answers for the last question include watching over us, hearing us when we pray, dying on the cross for us, understanding how hard it is to be human, and forgiving our sins.)

<u>Key Idea</u>: The only way to get to heaven is to believe in Jesus and love him. Then, God will let us live in heaven with him someday.

Corresponding Music

The Singing Bible, Disc 4 – Track 14
Song Title: *"The Fruit of the Spirit"*

Jesus' Teachings

Fingerplay

Do the fingerplay *"If You Believe in Jesus"*. Focus on the sound and motion for the letter 'V'.

Key Idea: 'V' = put your hand on your voice box, feel the vibration in your throat, and say *V-V*

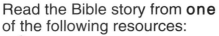

Bible Story

Read the Bible story from **one** of the following resources:

✔ Scripture: Luke 10:38-42

✔ *A Child's First Bible* p. 206-207

✔ *The New Bible in Pictures for Little Eyes* p. 284-285

Key Idea: Mary listened to Jesus.

Active Exploration

Provide an assortment of kitchen items for students to sort and stack. Have students count the number of items in each stack. Suggestions for kitchen items include the following: nonbreakable plates, bowls, cups, spoons, glasses, and napkins. You may also provide various containers with lids and have students match the lids to the containers.

Key Idea: Martha was too busy cooking to listen to Jesus. Mary stopped her work and listened.

Letter Activity

Copy the *Hide and Seek 'V'* page. Have students circle, color, highlight, or point to the 'V's' on the page. Younger students may need help in order to find any 'V's' at all. It is not necessary to find all the 'V's'. On the bottom of the page, have students connect 'V' to 'v' by tracing the dotted line from left to right.

Key Idea: Students should eventually recognize the capital and small letter 'V' within words.

Bible Activity

Copy *Count on Me* (in Appendix). Direct students to draw ears by making brown half-circles in each of the boxes. Younger students make 3 ears in each box. Older students make 4 ears in each box. Point to each ear as you count it. Write the numbers on the lines below each box as you count. Say the numbers below the boxes to count by 3's or by 4's (counting either '3', '6', '9' ... or '4', '8', '12' ...).

Key Idea: Jesus said it was good for Mary to take time to listen to him.

Corresponding Music

The Singing Bible, Disc 4 – Track 14
Song Title: *"The Fruit of the Spirit"*

Jesus' Teachings

Fingerplay

Do the fingerplay *"If You Believe in Jesus"*. Focus on the sound and motion for the letter 'V'.

Key Idea: 'V' = put your hand on your voice box, feel the vibration in your throat, and say *V-V*

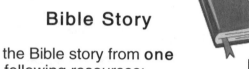

Bible Story

Read the Bible story from **one** of the following resources:

✔ Scripture: Luke 11:39-42

✔ *The New Bible in Pictures for Little Eyes* p. 286-287

Key Idea: Jesus talked to the Pharisees.

Devotional Activity

Read and discuss the devotion from **one** of the following resources:

✔ *Big Thoughts for Little People*
Read the two pages for letter 'V'.

✔ *Teach Them to Your Children*
Read the two pages for letter 'V'.

✔ *My ABC Bible Verses*
Read the two pages for letter 'V'.

Key Idea: Share a devotional focusing on character traits or memory work based on the letter 'V'.

Letter Activity

Use the 'V' flashcard from the Appendix. Have students trace the capital and small letter 'V's on the flashcard with their fingers. Using the flashcard as a model, choose either sidewalk chalk or 2 crayons taped together and paper to write more 'V's'.

Key Idea: Practice the motions needed to make the letter 'V'.

Bible Activity

Have students take turns pointing to things and naming them to show that everything we have belongs to God. Some possible items to name include the following: clothing, furniture, household items, toys, and things seen by looking out the window. Give students coins to practice putting in a dish like we put money in the offering plate at church.

Key Idea: God owns all that we have. We don't want to be like the Pharisees and be greedy and selfish.

Corresponding Music

The Singing Bible, Disc 4 – Track 14
Song Title: *"The Fruit of the Spirit"*

Hide and Seek 'V'

If you believe in Jesus

Spin around.

If Jesus hears your voice

Touch the ground.

V... V... V... V...

V _____ V

V _____ V

Jesus' Teachings

Fingerplay

Do the fingerplay *"If You Believe in Jesus"*. Focus on the sound and motion for the letter 'V'.

<u>Key Idea</u>: 'V' = put your hand on your voice box, feel the vibration in your throat, and say *V-V*

Bible Story

Read the Bible story from **one** of the following resources:

✔ Scripture: Luke 12:22, 27-31

✔ *The New Bible in Pictures for Little Eyes* p. 290-291

<u>Key Idea</u>: Jesus said not to worry.

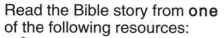

Art Activity

Tape 3 **crayons** together, making sure that the tips of the crayons are even with one another. Make several sets of taped crayons using a variety of colors. Tape a piece of **green paper** to the table for each student. Have students use the taped crayons to draw flowers in a field using circle and line motions. Have students use both the pointed and flat ends of the crayons.

<u>Key Idea</u>: We should not worry. God will care for all our needs, just as He cares for the flowers.

Letter Activity

Use masking tape to make a large 'V' on the floor. Have students place blocks on the tape to trace the letter. Each time a block is placed on the tape, students make the letter **sound**.

<u>Key Idea</u>: Each letter has a name and a sound, just like animals do. For example, a pig may be named Pinky, but it makes the sound, *Oink.*

Bible Activity

Have students be flowers. Give them the following directions: *Lift your arms and faces up to the sun. Sway back and forth in the wind. Bounce up and down as the rain hits your petals. Stomp as your roots pull water up out of the ground. Kneel down and roll up in a ball as the weather gets cold. Sleep during the winter. Slowly stand up and reach your arms toward the sun as spring comes again.*

<u>Key Idea</u>: We should be like the flowers, trusting God for our needs.

Corresponding Music

The Singing Bible, Disc 4 – Track 14
Song Title: *"The Fruit of the Spirit"*

Jesus' Ministry Continues

Fingerplay

Do the fingerplay *"Jesus Wipes Your Sins Clean"*. Focus on the sound and motion for the letter 'W'.

Key Idea: 'W' = move your hand in a circular motion and say *W-W*

Bible Story

Read the Bible story from **one** of the following resources:

✔ Scripture: Mark 9:2-4, 7-8
✔ *A Child's First Bible* p. 196-197
✔ *The New Bible in Pictures for Little Eyes* p. 298-299

Key Idea: God spoke from heaven.

Art Activity

Give each student a piece of **white paper**. Have students use **crayons** to draw and color a dark mountain with a bright yellow cloud on top.

Put **cooking oil** or **baby oil** on a **cotton ball** or wadded up **paper towel**. Tell students to rub the oil on the back of the drawing to make it transparent.

Key Idea: God's light from heaven shown on Jesus, making his clothes very bright and shiny.

Letter Activity

Copy the 'W' flashcard found in the Appendix. Show the letter side of the flashcard to the students. Read the *Hint* aloud. Demonstrate the motion and sound for 'W'. Have the students repeat it.

Key Idea: Students should eventually do the motion and say the sound for each flashcard without needing a *Hint* or a demonstration from you.

Bible Activity

Get out a white towel, a flashlight, and 3 stuffed toys. Have the students pretend to be Peter, James, or John on the mountain with Jesus. Set a stuffed toy on the table to represent Jesus on the mountain. Shine the flashlight on "Jesus" and add 2 more stuffed toys to the table to represent Moses and Elijah. Cover all 3 toys with the white towel to represent the cloud that covered Jesus. Pretend to be God's voice and say, *This is my Son whom I love. Listen to Him!* (Mark 9:7)

Key Idea: God said that Jesus is his Son, and we should do what He says.

Corresponding Music

None this lesson

Fingerplay: Jesus Wipes Your Sins Clean
(Sing to the tune of *"Jesus Loves Me"*)

Jesus tells you what to do.	*Point up*
Love our God as He loves you.	*Cross arms on chest*
Jesus watches over you.	*Shade eyes with hand*
He died taking blame for you.	*Hold index fingers in cross shape*
He *w-wipes* your sins clean.	*Make circular wiping motion*
He *w-wipes* your sins clean.	*Make circular wiping motion*
He *w-wipes* your sins clean.	*Make circular wiping motion*
Always tell him, *Thank you.*	*Fold hands to pray*

Jesus' Ministry Continues

Fingerplay

Do the fingerplay *"Jesus Wipes Your Sins Clean"*. Focus on the sound and motion for the letter 'W'.

Key Idea: 'W' = move your hand in a circular motion and say *W-W*

Letter Activity

Write a big 'W' on a piece of paper. Have students glue cotton balls or pieces of yarn to the letter. Younger students will need you to apply drops of glue on the letter for them first.

Key Idea: Students will become familiar with the shape and appearance of the capital letter 'W'.

Bible Story

Read the Bible story from **one** of the following resources:

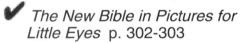

✔ Scripture: Luke 18:15-17

✔ *A Child's First Bible* p. 202-203

✔ *The New Bible in Pictures for Little Eyes* p. 302-303

Key Idea: Children came to Jesus.

Bible Activity

Act out the Bible story. You be a disciple, have the students be Jesus, and have stuffed toys or other figures be the children. Put the toys on the floor around "Jesus". Say, *No, Jesus is too busy to talk to children.* Have Jesus say, *Let the children come to me.* Have the students act like Jesus as they take turns picking up one stuffed toy at a time, holding it, patting it, hugging it and setting it back on the floor. Do this until all the stuffed toys have had a turn on "Jesus" lap.

Key Idea: Jesus is never too busy to talk to you, even if you are a little child. He loves you.

Devotional Activity

Read and discuss the devotion from **one** of the following resources:

✔ *Big Thoughts for Little People*
Read the two pages for letter 'W'.

✔ *Teach Them to Your Children*
Read the two pages for letter 'W'.

✔ *My ABC Bible Verses*
Read the two pages for letter 'W'.

Key Idea: Share a devotional focusing on character traits or memory work based on the letter 'W'.

Corresponding Music

The Singing Bible, Disc 4 – Track 7
Song Title: *"Two Commands"*

Jesus' Ministry Continues

Fingerplay

Do the fingerplay *"Jesus Wipes Your Sins Clean"*. Focus on the sound and motion for the letter 'W'.

Key Idea: 'W' = move your hand in a circular motion and say *W-W*

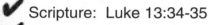

Bible Story

Read the Bible story from **one** of the following resources:

✔ Scripture: Luke 13:34-35

✔ *The New Bible in Pictures for Little Eyes* p. 304-305

Key Idea: The people in Jerusalem made Jesus sad.

Dramatic Play

Have students build a city out of blocks, boxes, or Legos. Little toy people may be added to the city. Tell students ahead of time that the city, Jerusalem, will be knocked down by an army. After the city is completed, have students stand up, march from a distance toward the city, and knock it down. Ask, *Why did the city get knocked down?*

Key Idea: Jesus was sad because He knew Jerusalem would be destroyed one day.

Letter Activity

Copy the *Hide and Seek 'W'* page. Have students circle, color, highlight, or point to the 'W's' on the page. Younger students may need help in order to find any 'W's' at all. It is not necessary to find all the 'W's'. On the bottom of the page, have students connect 'W' to 'w' by tracing the dotted line from left to right.

Key Idea: Students should eventually recognize the capital and small letter 'W' within words.

Bible Activity

Copy the *GRAY is...* page. Have students find gray items in a magazine or a catalog to cut out. Use a marker to circle, box, or outline the gray items, so that students have a line to follow as they cut. Have students glue the items on the *GRAY is...* page. Save this page. A page will be added each week to make a color book.

Key Idea: Gray is for Jerusalem's walls. Many Jews in Jerusalem didn't believe Jesus was God's Son.

Corresponding Music

The Singing Bible, Disc 4 – Track 7
Song Title: *"Two Commands"*

Hide and Seek 'W'

Jesus tells you what to do.

Love our God as He loves you.

Jesus watches over you.

He died, taking blame for you.

W... W... W...

W_____ w

W_____ w

GRAY is...

for Jerusalem's walls.

Jesus' Ministry Continues

Fingerplay

Do the fingerplay *"Jesus Wipes Your Sins Clean"*. Focus on the sound and motion for the letter 'W'.

Key Idea: 'W' = move your hand in a circular motion and say *W-W*

Letter Activity

Use masking tape to make a large 'W' on the floor. Have students drive a toy car or other toy vehicle on the tape to trace the letter. Have students say the letter **sound** as they drive.

Key Idea: Each letter has a name and a sound, just like animals do.
For example, a bunny may be named Cottontail, but it makes the sound, *Squeak.*

Bible Story

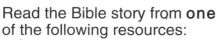

Read the Bible story from **one** of the following resources:

✔ Scripture: John 12:2-3 and Luke 21:1-4

✔ *A Child's First Bible* p. 200-201 (plus the Scripture listed above)

✔ *The New Bible in Pictures for Little Eyes* p. 308-309, 318-319

Key Idea: Give to the Lord.

Bible Activity

Copy *Count on Me* (in Appendix). Direct students to draw perfume bottles by making purple ovals that each have a smaller oval on top in the boxes. Younger students make 3 bottles in each box. Older students make 4 bottles in each box. Point to each bottle as you count it. Write the numbers on the lines below each box as you count. Say the numbers below the boxes to count by 3's or by 4's (counting either '3', '6', '9' ... or '4', '8', '12' ...).

Key Idea: The woman poured perfume on Jesus' feet to show love.

Math Activity

Youngers: Use 5 index cards. Draw colored dots on each card to show the numbers '1-5'. Help students count and place coins one at a time on each dot on the cards.
Olders: Use 10 index cards. Write one number from '1-10' on each card. Place pennies on each card to match the number. Trade 5 pennies for a nickel and 10 for a dime.

Key Idea: The widow in the story gave all her money to the Lord.

Corresponding Music

The Singing Bible, Disc 4 – Track 7
Song Title: *"Two Commands"*

Jesus' Ministry Continues

Fingerplay

Do the fingerplay *"Jesus Wipes Your Sins Clean"*. Focus on the sound and motion for the letter 'W'.

Key Idea: 'W' = move your hand in a circular motion and say *W-W*

Letter Activity

Use the 'W' flashcard from the Appendix. Have students trace the capital and small letter 'W' on the flashcard with their fingers. Using the flashcard as a model, give students either a small amount of cooking oil or liquid soap on an aluminum pan or plate to use to write more 'W's'.

Key Idea: Practice the motions needed to make the letter 'W'.

Bible Story

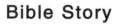
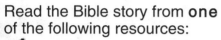

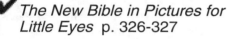

Read the Bible story from **one** of the following resources:

✔ Scripture: Matthew 22:34-39

✔ *A Child's First Bible* p. 184-185 (plus the Scripture listed above)

✔ *The New Bible in Pictures for Little Eyes* p. 326-327

Key Idea: The greatest command is to love.

Bible Activity

Discuss loving God with all your heart, your soul, and your mind. (Matthew 22:37) For example, we must know about God in our minds, want to obey him in our hearts, and try to obey him with the Holy Spirit's help.

Discuss what it means to love your neighbor as yourself. (Matt. 22:39) For example, treat your neighbor the way you want to be treated. These 2 commands sum up the Ten Commandments.

Key Idea: Jesus tells us how God wants us to live our lives.

Active Exploration

Walk around, opening and closing drawers, doors, cupboards, and hampers. Have students say either *open* or *closed* as you open and close each item. Set out a Bible, a lidded container, a can, a tube of toothpaste, and a few books. Open some of the items and leave the rest closed. Students say which items are closed and which are open.

Key Idea: The Bible must be opened and read to know what God says to us.

Corresponding Music

The Singing Bible, Disc 4 – Track 7
Song Title: *"Two Commands"*

Preparing for Jesus' Death

Fingerplay

Do the fingerplay *"X Marks the Spot"*. Focus on the sound and motion for the letter 'X'.

Key Idea: 'X' = make an 'X' using two index fingers and say *X-X*

Bible Story

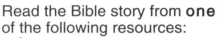

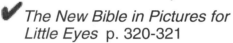

Read the Bible story from **one** of the following resources:

✔ Scripture: Luke 19:32-38

✔ *A Child's First Bible* p. 218-219

✔ *The New Bible in Pictures for Little Eyes* p. 320-321

Key Idea: Jesus rode a donkey into Jerusalem.

Dramatic Play

Supply several large coats with big buttons, velcro, snaps, and zippers. Students practice putting the coats on until they can do it on their own. Help students learn to velcro, button, snap, and zip. Last, students practice taking the coats off and laying them on the ground, like the people did for Jesus in the story.

Key Idea: People put their coats down to honor Jesus as He rode by on his donkey.

Letter Activity

Copy the 'X' flashcard found in the Appendix. Show the letter side of the flashcard to the students. Read the *Hint* aloud. Demonstrate the motion and sound for 'X'. Have the students repeat it.

Key Idea: Students should eventually do the motion and say the sound for each flashcard without needing a *Hint* or a demonstration.

Bible Activity

Copy the *GREEN is...* page. Have students find green items in a magazine or a catalog to cut out. Use a marker to circle, box, or outline the green items, so that students have a line to follow as they cut. Have students glue the items on the *GREEN is...* page. Staple together the pages that you saved from the previous weeks to make a color book.

Key Idea: Green is for the palm branches that the people waved as Jesus rode into Jerusalem. They thought Jesus was going to be their earthly king.

Corresponding Music

The Singing Bible, Disc 4 – Track 6
Song Title: *"The Lord's Prayer"*

Fingerplay: 'X' Marks the Spot

Days 1-5

Jesus knows	*Point to head*
What is to come.	
God's will	*Bow head, fold hands*
Must be done.	
He could leave	*Walk fingers up arm quickly*
Or run away.	
But...	
'X' marks the spot	*Make 'X' with index fingers*
Where Jesus waits.	*Hands next to legs*
X... X... X...	*Make 'X' with index fingers*

Jesus knows	*Point to head*
What is to come.	
God's will	*Bow head, fold hands*
Must be done.	
Judas' soldiers	*Walk fingers up arm quickly*
Take him away.	
But...	
'X' marks the spot	*Make 'X' with index fingers*
Where Jesus waits.	*Hands next to legs*
X... X... X...	*Make 'X' with index fingers*

GREEN is...

for the palm branches that
the people waved as Jesus rode into Jerusalem.

Preparing for Jesus' Death

Fingerplay

Do the fingerplay *"X Marks the Spot"*. Focus on the sound and motion for the letter 'X'.

Key Idea: 'X' = make an 'X' using two index fingers and say *X-X*

Letter Activity

Write a big 'X' on a piece of paper. Have students glue dried macaroni or raisins to the letter. Younger students will need you to apply drops of glue on the letter for them first.

Key Idea: Students will become familiar with the shape and appearance of the capital letter 'X'.

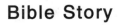

Bible Story

Read the Bible story from **one** of the following resources:

✔ Scripture: Mark 14:17-25
✔ *A Child's First Bible* p. 220-221
✔ *The New Bible in Pictures for Little Eyes* p. 328-329

Key Idea: They had the Last Supper.

Bible Activity

Set out a small tub of water, a towel, torn pieces of bread, and red juice. (If you don't have red juice, add red food coloring to a different kind of juice.) Explain that we need to be reverent as we discuss the "Last Supper" because what Jesus did and said was very important. Say, *Jesus washed his disciples' feet to show them they must serve others.* Wash the students' feet. Discuss how we can serve others. Give each student a small piece of bread and a small cup of red drink. Explain what communion means according to Mark 14:22-24.

Key Idea: Jesus taught us how to remember him and serve him.

Devotional Activity

Read and discuss the devotion from **one** of the following resources:

✔ *Big Thoughts for Little People*
Read the two pages for letter 'X'.
✔ *Teach Them to Your Children*
Read the two pages for letter 'X'.
✔ *My ABC Bible Verses*
Read the two pages for letter 'X'.

Key Idea: Share a devotional focusing on character traits or memory work based on the letter 'X'.

Corresponding Music

The Singing Bible, Disc 4 – Track 6
Song Title: *"The Lord's Prayer"*

Preparing for Jesus' Death

Fingerplay

Do the fingerplay *"X Marks the Spot"*. Focus on the sound and motion for the letter 'X'.

Key Idea: 'X' = make an 'X' using two index fingers and say *X-X*

Letter Activity

Use the 'X' flashcard from the Appendix. Have students trace the capital and small letter 'X' on the flashcard with their fingers. Using the flashcard as a model, choose either pudding, chocolate syrup, baby food, or fingerpaint on a plate, pan, or piece of paper for students to write more 'X's'.

Key Idea: Practice the motions needed to make the letter 'X'.

Bible Story

Read the Bible story from **one** of the following resources:

✔ Scripture: John 14:1-7

✔ *The New Bible in Pictures for Little Eyes* p. 330-331

Key Idea: Jesus talked about heaven.

Bible Activity

Read the following list of Scriptures and discuss what they tell us about heaven: Heaven will be a happy place. (Rev. 21:4, 27) Jesus has prepared a place for us. (John 14:2) We will never be hungry or thirsty. (Rev. 7:16) Heaven will be very beautiful. (Rev. 21:21, 22:1-2) All animals will live in peace. (Isa. 11:6-7) It is never night. (Rev. 22:5) Our heavenly bodies will be glorious. (1 Cor. 15:40) A day in heaven is like 1,000 years on earth. (Psalm 90:4)

Key Idea: If we believe in Jesus, we will be in heaven someday with him.

Math Activity

Youngers: Discuss and list on paper what the students did yesterday. Discuss and list what the students are doing today, and then guess and list what will happen tomorrow.
Olders: Do the same activity using the general terms past, present, and future.

Key Idea: Only the Lord knows the future. We must believe in him and be ready for his return, because we never know when He may come to take us to heaven.

Corresponding Music

The Singing Bible, Disc 4 – Track 6
Song Title: *"The Lord's Prayer"*

Preparing for Jesus' Death

Fingerplay

Do the fingerplay *"X Marks the Spot"*. Focus on the sound and motion for the letter 'X'.

Key Idea: 'X' = make an 'X' using two index fingers and say *X-X*

Bible Story

Read the Bible story from **one** of the following resources:

✔ Scripture: Luke 22:41-51, Matthew 26:53-54

✔ *A Child's First Bible* p. 222-225

✔ *The New Bible in Pictures for Little Eyes* p. 332-335

Key Idea: Judas betrayed Jesus.

Art Activity

Wrap and tape a piece of **aluminum foil** over a sheet of **paper**. Have students use **Q-tips** and **paint** to paint a nighttime garden scene on the aluminum foil. Have students use a different Q-tip for each color of paint. Possible suggestions for objects to paint include the following: trees, flowers, grass, stream, and rocks.

Key Idea: Jesus prayed to God in the garden on the night He was taken away by the soldiers.

Letter Activity

Use masking tape to make a large 'X' on the floor. Have students tiptoe on the tape to trace the letter. Then, have students jump off the end of the letter saying the letter **sound** as they jump.

Key Idea: Each letter has a name and a sound, just like animals do. For example, a lamb may be named Whitey, but it makes the sound, *Baa.*

Bible Activity

Have students choose props to represent Jesus, the garden, the soldiers, and Judas. Read the following directions for students to act out with their chosen props: *Shut the lights off, so it is night. Show Jesus kneeling and praying in the garden. Have Jesus wait as Judas comes toward him with the soldiers. Make Judas kiss Jesus on the cheek to show the soldiers who to arrest. Lead Jesus away.*

Key Idea: Jesus did God's will, even though He didn't have to do it.

Corresponding Music

The Singing Bible, Disc 4 – Track 6
Song Title: *"The Lord's Prayer"*

Preparing for Jesus' Death

Fingerplay

Do the fingerplay *"X Marks the Spot"*. Focus on the sound and motion for the letter 'X'.

Key Idea: 'X' = make an 'X' using two index fingers and say *X-X*

Bible Story

Read the Bible story from **one** of the following resources:

✔ Scripture: Luke 22:59-62

✔ *A Child's First Bible* p. 226-227

✔ *The New Bible in Pictures for Little Eyes* p. 336-337

Key Idea: Peter said he didn't know Jesus.

Active Exploration

Have students sit in pairs facing one another with their legs open. Set a timer for 1 minute and have partners roll a ball back and forth to each other. When the timer rings, the person without the ball points at the other person. The person with the ball says, *Jesus is my friend.* Scoot farther apart and repeat the game. Older students stand and toss the ball, rather than rolling it.

Key Idea: Peter was Jesus' friend, but he said he didn't know Jesus.

Letter Activity

Copy the *Hide and Seek 'X'* page. Have students circle, color, highlight, or point to the 'X's on the page. Younger students may need help in order to find any 'X's at all. It is not necessary to find all the 'X's. On the bottom of the page, have students connect 'X' to 'x' by tracing the dotted line from left to right.

Key Idea: Students should eventually recognize the capital and small letter 'X' within words.

Bible Activity

Copy *Count on Me* (in Appendix). Direct students to draw sad mouths by making red upside-down smiles in the boxes. Younger students make 3 mouths in each box. Older students make 4 mouths in each box. Point to each mouth as you count it. Write the numbers on the lines below each box as you count. Say the numbers below the boxes to count by 3's or by 4's (counting either '3', '6', '9' ... or '4', '8', '12' ...).

Key Idea: Peter lied about knowing Jesus.

Corresponding Music

The Singing Bible, Disc 4 – Track 6
Song Title: *"The Lord's Prayer"*

Hide and Seek 'X'

He could leave or run away.

But, 'X' marks the spot

Where Jesus waits.

X... X... X...

Jesus' Crucifixion and Resurrection

Fingerplay

Do the fingerplay *"What Do You Know?"* Focus on reviewing the sounds and motions for the letters.

Key Idea: Practice the sounds and motions for the letters 'A-X'.

Bible Story

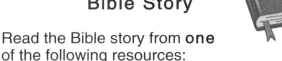

Read the Bible story from **one** of the following resources:

✔ Scripture: Mark 15:6-15

✔ *A Child's First Bible* p. 228-229

✔ *The New Bible in Pictures for Little Eyes* p. 338-339

Key Idea: Pilate followed the crowd.

Active Exploration

Go on a journey through a forest by doing the listed actions. Actions for going the right way are hard work. (i.e. climb trees, swing on vines, jump over tree roots, and walk uphill) Actions for going the wrong way have consequences. (i.e trip over rocks, roll down a hill, sink into quicksand, fall into a swamp, get stuck in mud) Make sure to point out whether actions are going the right way or the wrong way.

Key Idea: Doing the right thing isn't always easy, but it is better.

Letter Activity

This is a review week. Review all the flashcards from the previous weeks. Show the letter side of each flashcard to the students. Have them respond with the motion and sound. If needed, read the *Hint* or demonstrate the motion and sound.

Key Idea: Students should eventually do the motion and say the sound for each flashcard without needing a *Hint* or a demonstration.

Bible Activity

Copy *Count on Me* (in Appendix). Direct students to draw patches of darkness by coloring black rectangles in each of the boxes. Younger students make 3 dark patches in each box. Older students make 4 dark patches in each box. Point to each patch of darkness as you count. Write the numbers on the lines below each box as you count. Say the numbers below the boxes to count by 3's or by 4's (counting either '3', '6', '9' ... or '4', '8', '12' ...).

Key Idea: Pilate sent Jesus to the cross, even though he knew Jesus had done nothing wrong.

Corresponding Music

The Singing Bible, Disc 4 – Track 6
Song Title: *"The Lord's Prayer"*

Fingerplay: What Do You Know?

We've learned about *A-A-Adam*	*Hands on cheeks in surprise*
And *B-B-Boat,*	*Hug yourself and rock side-to-side*
C-C-Clippity clop	*Tap palms on thighs in rhythm*
And *D-D-Dusty* camel.	*Hold reins of camel and move up-down-up-down*
E-E-Empty jars	*Shake hand to shake empty jar*
And *F-F-Fire,*	*Wiggle 10 fingers like flames*
G-G-Gurgle	*Hold nose, put hand up*
And *H-H-Helping* hands.	*Lace fingers, move up and down*
I-Impossible	*Push palms up as if lifting*
And *J-J-Joyful* jumping,	*2 fingers jump on palm of hand*
K-K-clapping hands	*Clap hands above head*
And *L-L-La-La-La.*	*Swing hand back and forth*
M-M-Miracles	*Pat hand over mouth, pull it away*
And *N-N-Naughty* king,	*Tap top of hand with 2 fingers*
O-O-Off	*Brush one hand with the other*
And *P-P-Pulling* oars.	*Make fists and pull them in*
Q-Q-Quivering	*Shake whole body*
And *R-R-Ready* to choose,	*Hold chin with hand, thinking*
S-S-Storms blowing	*Cover ears*
And *T-Time* to move.	*Tap wrist with finger, jump up*

Fingerplay: What Do You Know?
(continued)

Days 1-5

U-U, Uh-Uh	*Shake head, "No"*
And *V-V-Voice,*	*Touch throat with hand*
W-Wipe sins away	*Make circular wiping motion*
And *X-X* marks the spot.	*Make 'X' with index fingers*
Now, as Jesus	*Point up*
Is put on the cross,	*Make cross symbol with arms*
He is perfect.	*Point up*
But, He dies for us.	*Point to self*
Just like the others	*Open palms together like Bible*
God has plans for you too.	*Point up, then point to yourself*
Never forget	*Shake head, "No"*
What God can do!	*Spread arms wide*

Jesus' Crucifixion and Resurrection

Fingerplay

Do the fingerplay *"What Do You Know?"* Focus on reviewing the sounds and motions for the letters.

Key Idea: Practice the sounds and motions for the letters 'A-X'.

Letter Activity

Choose one or more of the letters 'A-X' to review. Use masking tape to make the large review letter on the floor. Have students sit on a pillow and scoot on the tape to trace the letter. Have students say the letter **sound** as they scoot.

Key Idea: Each letter has a name and a sound, just like animals do. For example, a bird may be named Robin, but it makes the sound, *Chirp.*

Bible Story

Read the Bible story from **one** of the following resources:

✔ Scripture: Luke 23:33-35, 44-46

✔ *A Child's First Bible* p. 230-231

✔ *The New Bible in Pictures for Little Eyes* p. 340-341

Key Idea: Jesus died on the cross.

Bible Activity

Have students share sins from the last few days. Explain that Jesus died to forgive those sins, so we won't have to go to hell. Those sins are forgiven if we just ask Jesus. Ask students, *Would you want to take a spank for someone else? Jesus did much more than that, He died for us.* Lead students in a prayer to ask for forgiveness and to thank Jesus for dying on the cross.

Key Idea: Jesus suffered for our sins by dying on the cross.

Art Activity

Give each student one sheet of **black paper**. Students may use **white chalk, white crayon,** or **white paper** to make three crosses on a hill on the black paper. Students should <u>not</u> use any other colors in this picture. Explain to students that the black shows sadness, but the white shows the hope we have in Jesus.

Key Idea: It was very sad when Jesus died. He did this so that we have hope that we are forgiven and may go to heaven someday.

Corresponding Music

The Singing Bible, Disc 4 – Track 6
Song Title: *"The Lord's Prayer"*

Jesus' Crucifixion and Resurrection

Fingerplay

Do the fingerplay *"What Do You Know?"* Focus on reviewing the sounds and motions for the letters.

Key Idea: Practice the sounds and motions for the letters 'A-X'.

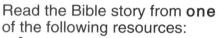

Bible Story

Read the Bible story from **one** of the following resources:

 Scripture: Matthew 27:57-60

 A Child's First Bible p. 232

 The New Bible in Pictures for Little Eyes p. 342-343

Key Idea: Jesus was in the tomb.

Math Activity

Youngers: Place a bowl on its side to represent the place where Jesus' body was laid. Put up to 10 items in the bowl. Say, *There is more than 1 item in the bowl.* Have students count and remove items one at a time until only one is left all alone. Olders: Change the activity above by counting the total number of items first and then counting backwards, removing items one at a time until one is left all alone.

Key Idea: Jesus' body was wrapped and laid in the tomb all alone.

Letter Activity

Choose one letter from 'A-X' to review. Write that letter on a big piece of paper. Use water to thin glue and have students "paint" the glue on the letter. Then, sprinkle either salt, coffee grounds, glitter, or any kind of spice on the glue. Younger students will need you to help them with the sprinkling part.

Key Idea: Students will become familiar with the shape and appearance of the capital letters.

Bible Activity

Discuss the following questions with the students: *Did Jesus really die? How do we know? Is Jesus still dead? Why isn't Jesus dead anymore? Where is Jesus now? Will we ever get to see Jesus? How do we know we will see Jesus someday?*

Key Idea: Jesus died on the cross. His body was wrapped up and put in the tomb. But, Jesus didn't stay in the tomb.

Corresponding Music

None this lesson

Jesus' Crucifixion and Resurrection

Fingerplay

Do the fingerplay *"What Do You Know?"* Focus on reviewing the sounds and motions for the letters.

Key Idea: Practice the sounds and motions for the letters 'A-X'.

Bible Story

Read the Bible story from **one** of the following resources:

✔ Scripture: Matthew 28:1-7
✔ *A Child's First Bible* p. 233
✔ *The New Bible in Pictures for Little Eyes* p. 344-345

Key Idea: Jesus rose.

Devotional Activity

Read and discuss the devotion from **one** of the following resources:

✔ *Big Thoughts for Little People*
Review verses for 'U', 'V', 'W', 'X'
✔ *Teach Them to Your Children*
Review verses for 'U, 'V', 'W', 'X'
✔ *My ABC Bible Verses*
Review verses for 'U', 'V', 'W', 'X'

Key Idea: Share a devotional focusing on character traits or memory work based on the letters 'U', 'V', 'W', 'X'.

Letter Activity

Copy the *Hide and Seek Review* page. Choose a letter from 'U-X' to review. Have students circle, color, highlight, or point to the chosen letter. Younger students may need help in order to find any of the chosen letters. On the bottom of the page, have students draw a line to connect each capital letter to its matching lowercase letter.

Key Idea: Students should eventually recognize the capital and small letters 'U-X' within words.

Bible Activity

Give each student a piece of paper. Help students complete each of the following directions one at a time: Draw a brown circle at the top of the page to be a stone. Color yellow on the left side of the page to be a bright light. Draw a red smile on the right side of the page.

Key Idea: An angel at the tomb told the women who came to visit Jesus' body that He wasn't there. The women were happy! He was alive!

Corresponding Music

The Singing Bible, Disc 4 – Track 8
Song Titles: *"Easter Song"*

Hide and Seek Review

We've learned about Uh-Uh

And V-V-Voice,

W-W-Wipe sins away

And X-X marks the spot.

U

W

V

u

W

v

X

x

Jesus' Crucifixion and Resurrection

Fingerplay

Do the fingerplay *"What Do You Know?"* Focus on reviewing the sounds and motions for the letters.

Key Idea: Practice the sounds and motions for the letters 'A-X'.

Bible Story

Read the Bible story from **one** of the following resources:

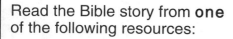 Scripture: Matthew 28:8-10

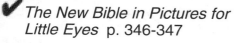 *The New Bible in Pictures for Little Eyes* p. 346-347

Key Idea: The women saw Jesus.

Dramatic Play

Turn the lights off. Youngers: Shine a flashlight on an object and have the students name it. Allow the students to have a turn shining the flashlight as well.
Olders: Describe an object and have the students shine the flashlight on the object being described. Allow the students a turn to describe an object for you to find as well.

Key Idea: The women saw Jesus and knew it was him.

Letter Activity

Choose one or more of the flashcards from the previous weeks to review. Have students trace the capital and small letters on the flashcards with their fingers. Using the flashcards as models, choose either markers and markerboards or pieces of carpet and fingers to practice writing more letters.

Key Idea: Practice the motions needed to make the letters.

Bible Activity

Act out the Bible story. You pretend to be Jesus. Have the students pretend to be the women in the story. The women hurry away from the tomb with smiles on their faces. They meet Jesus, act surprised, and bow down at his feet to worship him. Tell the women not to be afraid and to tell his disciples to meet him in Galilee.

Key Idea: Jesus met the women on the road. He gave them a message for his disciples.

Corresponding Music

The Singing Bible, Disc 4 – Track 8
Song Titles: *"Easter Song"*

Jesus' Resurrection and Ascension

Fingerplay

Do the fingerplay *"Jesus Is Alive"*. Focus on the sound and motion for the letter 'Y'.

Key Idea: 'Y'= punch fist in the air and say *Y-Y*

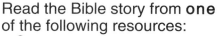

Bible Story

Read the Bible story from **one** of the following resources:

✔ Scripture: John 20:6-9

✔ *The New Bible in Pictures for Little Eyes* p. 348-351

Key Idea: Peter and John saw that the grave was empty.

Active Exploration

Set out items that are full and items that are empty. Have students point out which are full and which are empty. Possible full items include a box of food, kleenex box, tub of toys, can of food, box of crayons, roll of tape, glue stick, tube of toothpaste, and a bottle of shampoo. Possible empty items include a glass, cup, food storage container, bowl, pot, laundry basket, box, and paper bag.

Key Idea: Jesus' grave was empty. His body was gone and the cloths were still lying there.

Letter Activity

Copy the 'Y' flashcard found in the Appendix. Show the letter side of the flashcard to the students. Read the *Hint* aloud. Demonstrate the motion and sound for 'Y'. Have the students repeat it.

Key Idea: Students should eventually do the motion and say the sound for each flashcard without needing a *Hint* or a demonstration from you.

Bible Activity

Copy *Count on Me* (in Appendix). Direct students to draw stones by making brown colored circles in each of the boxes. Younger students make 3 stones in each box. Older students make 4 stones in each box. Point to each stone as you count it with the students. Write the numbers on the lines below each box as you count. Say the numbers below the boxes to count by 3's or by 4's (counting either '3', '6', '9' ... or '4', '8', '12' ...).

Key Idea: The stone was rolled away, and the tomb was empty. Jesus wasn't there anymore.

Corresponding Music

The Singing Bible, Disc 4 – Track 8
Song Title: *"Easter Song"*

Fingerplay: Jesus Is Alive

Hurry to the grave.

Faster they go.   *Run in place quickly*

Jesus isn't there.

Leave so slow.   *Walk in place slowly*

He is alive!

Clap your hands.   *Clap hands*

He rose for you and me.

Shout *y-yeah!*   *Punch fist in the air twice*

Jesus sees his friends.

Jump two times.   *Leap in the air twice*

He goes up to heaven.

Reach up high.   *Kneel down and slowly rise*

God knows we're alone.

Tiptoe very slow.   *Tiptoe around slowly*

He sends his spirit down.

Reach down low.   *Reach down to the ground*

Jesus' Resurrection and Ascension

Fingerplay

Do the fingerplay *"Jesus Is Alive"*. Focus on the sound and motion for the letter 'Y'.

Key Idea: 'Y'= punch fist in the air and say *Y-Y*

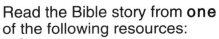

Bible Story

Read the Bible story from **one** of the following resources:

✔ Scripture: Mark 16:12-13

✔ *The New Bible in Pictures for Little Eyes* p. 352-353

Key Idea: Two men saw Jesus.

Dramatic Play

Choose 3 toys with varying textures (i.e. a stuffed toy, a toy with wheels, and a smooth toy such as a Lincoln log or tinker toy). Show the 3 toys to the students. Have students close their eyes. Rub one toy on each student's arm, leg, or back. Have the students guess which toy was used. Ask, *How did you guess which toy was used?* Switch roles and allow the students to rub the toy on your arm, leg, or back instead.

Key Idea: The men didn't know who was walking with them, but then they realized it was Jesus.

Letter Activity

Write a big 'Y' on a piece of paper. Have students glue dry 'O'-shaped cereal or dried beans to the letter. Younger students will need you to apply drops of glue on the letter for them first.

Key Idea: Students will become familiar with the shape and appearance of the capital letter 'Y'.

Bible Activity

Ask students, *How do we talk to Jesus?* (by praying) *Does He hear us when we pray?* (The Bible tells us that Jesus hears us whenever we pray.) *What can we talk to Jesus about?* (Some possible examples include our fears, to give thanks, happy things, for help, sad times, or to say we're sorry.) Remind students that Jesus knows what it is like to live on earth. He has felt many of the same things that we feel. Say, *Let's talk to Jesus right now.*

Key Idea: We can talk to Jesus too, just like the men in the story did.

Corresponding Music

The Singing Bible, Disc 4 – Track 8 Song Title: *"Easter Song"*

Jesus' Resurrection and Ascension

Fingerplay

Do the fingerplay *"Jesus Is Alive"*. Focus on the sound and motion for the letter 'Y'.

<u>Key Idea</u>: 'Y'= punch fist in the air and say *Y-Y*

Bible Story

Read the Bible story from **one** of the following resources:

✔ Scripture: Luke 24:36-42

✔ *A Child's First Bible* p. 234

✔ *The New Bible in Pictures for Little Eyes* p. 354-355

<u>Key Idea</u>: The disciples saw Jesus.

Math Activity

<u>Youngers</u>: Have students practice holding up between one and five fingers and saying the matching number. <u>Olders</u>: Have students use fingers and toes to count up to ten or twenty and backwards from ten to one. Show addition by holding up fingers on one hand and fingers on the other hand for students to describe with an addition sentence.

<u>Key Idea</u>: Jesus showed the disciples his hands and feet, so they would know it was really him.

Letter Activity

Copy the *Hide and Seek 'Y'* page. Have students circle, color, highlight, or point to the 'Y's' on the page. Younger students may need help in order to find any 'Y's' at all. It is not necessary to find all the 'Y's'. On the bottom of the page, have students connect 'Y' to 'y' by tracing the dotted line from left to right.

<u>Key Idea</u>: Students should eventually recognize the capital and small letter 'Y' within words.

Bible Activity

Give each student a piece of paper. Help students complete each of the following directions one at a time: Trace around your hand at the top of the page. Color a red nail hole in the middle of the hand. Trace around your foot at the bottom of the page. Color a red nail hole in the middle of the foot.

<u>Key Idea</u>: Jesus visited the disciples and ate with them. He showed them the nail holes in his hands and feet and told them He was not a ghost.

Corresponding Music

The Singing Bible, Disc 4 – Track 8
Song Title: *"Easter Song"*

Hide and Seek 'Y'

He is alive!

Clap your hands.

He rose for you and me.

Shout y-yeah!

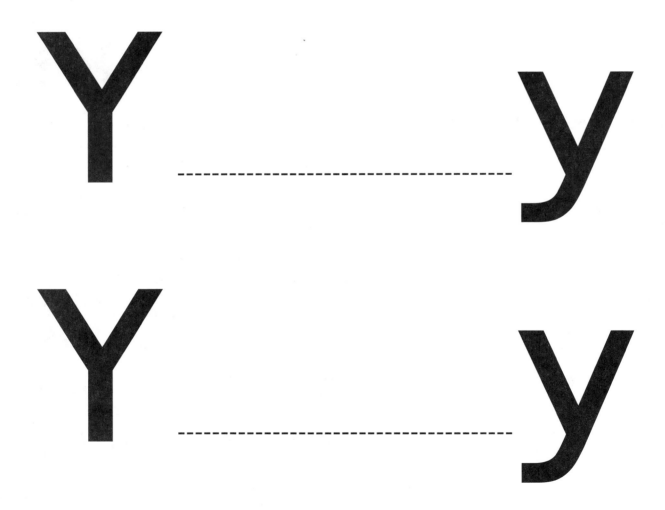

Jesus' Resurrection and Ascension

Fingerplay

Do the fingerplay *"Jesus Is Alive".*
Focus on the sound and motion for the letter 'Y'.

<u>Key Idea:</u> 'Y'= punch fist in the air and say *Y-Y*

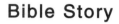

Bible Story

Read the Bible story from **one** of the following resources:

✔ Scripture: Acts 1:9-11

✔ *A Child's First Bible* p. 234-235

✔ *The New Bible in Pictures for Little Eyes* p. 356-357

<u>Key Idea:</u> Jesus went to heaven.

Devotional Activity

Read and discuss the devotion from **one** of the following resources:

✔ *Big Thoughts for Little People*
Read the two pages for letter 'Y'.

✔ *Teach Them to Your Children*
Read the two pages for letter 'Y'.

✔ *My ABC Bible Verses*
Read the two pages for letter 'Y'.

<u>Key Idea:</u> Share a devotional focusing on character traits or memory work based on the letter 'Y'.

Letter Activity

Use the 'Y' flashcard from the Appendix. Have students trace the capital and small letter 'Y's'' on the flashcard with their fingers. Using the flashcard as a model, choose either a bar of soap on a mirror or an ice cube on construction paper to write more 'Y's'.

<u>Key Idea:</u> Practice the motions needed to make the letter 'Y'.

Bible Activity

Set out 11 props to represent the disciples. Scatter them around on the floor. Place one prop in the center to be Jesus. Use a pillow or a blanket to represent the clouds. Cover "Jesus" with the "clouds" and have him rise up and disappear. Have the "disciples" look up in wonder. Then, use 2 props to be angels. The angels say, *Why are you looking up? Jesus will come back again someday this same way.*

<u>Key Idea:</u> Jesus went up to heaven. He will come back again someday and take his followers to heaven.

Corresponding Music

The Singing Bible, Disc 4 – Track 16
Song Title: *"Just Like Lightning"*

Jesus' Resurrection and Ascension

Fingerplay

Do the fingerplay *"Jesus Is Alive"*. Focus on the sound and motion for the letter 'Y'.

<u>Key Idea</u>: 'Y'= punch fist in the air and say *Y-Y*

Bible Story

Read the Bible story from **one** of the following resources:

✔ Scripture: Acts 2:1-3

✔ *A Child's First Bible* p. 236-237

✔ *The New Bible in Pictures for Little Eyes* p. 358-359

<u>Key Idea</u>: Jesus sent the Holy Spirit.

Art Activity

Give each student a **paper plate**. Have students **color** or **paint** both sides of the plate with red, yellow, and orange flames. **Cut** the plate around and around in a spiral motion so that it hangs in one curly strip. The strip represents a tongue of fire, like the Holy Spirit. Hang the strips from the ceiling to remind students about the Holy Spirit.

<u>Key Idea</u>: When Jesus went to heaven, He sent the Holy Spirit to be with us.

Letter Activity

Use masking tape to make a large 'Y' on the floor. Have students walk a stuffed animal on the tape to trace the letter. Then, have students walk the letter themselves, saying the letter **sound** as they walk.

<u>Key Idea</u>: Each letter has a name and a sound, just like animals do. For example, a duck may be named Ducky, but it makes the sound, *Quack*.

Bible Activity

Set out 12 props for the 12 disciples. (This includes Matthias who was the replacement for Judas.) Give students the following directions: Make the disciples kneel and pray. Make a loud noise like a rushing wind. Have the disciples look up. Use the art project from today to touch the top of each disciple's head with a tongue of fire. Point to each disciple's body to show where the Holy Spirit went.

<u>Key Idea</u>: The Holy Spirit came to the disciples as they were praying.

Corresponding Music

The Singing Bible, Disc 4 – Track 16
Song Title: *"Just Like Lightning"*

The Spread of the Gospel

Fingerplay

Do the fingerplay *"Zip! Zap! Zing!"* Focus on the sound and motion for the letter 'Z'.

<u>Key Idea</u>: 'Z' = snap fingers and say *Z-Z*

Letter Activity

Copy the 'Z' flashcard found in the Appendix. Show the letter side of the flashcard to the students. Read the *Hint* aloud. Demonstrate the motion and sound for 'Z'. Have the students repeat it.

<u>Key Idea</u>: Students should eventually do the motion and say the sound for each flashcard without needing a *Hint* or a demonstration from you.

Bible Story

Read the Bible story from **one** of the following resources:

✔ Scripture: Act 2:4-8, 36-38

✔ *A Child's First Bible* p. 242-243 (plus the Scripture listed above)

✔ *The New Bible in Pictures for Little Eyes* p. 360-361

<u>Key Idea</u>: Peter talked to the crowd.

Bible Activity

Copy *Count on Me* (in Appendix). Direct students to draw earths by making circles colored blue and green in each of the boxes. Younger students make 3 earths in each box. Older students make 4 earths in each box. Point to each earth as you count. Write the numbers on the lines below each box as you count. Say the numbers below the boxes to count by 3's or by 4's (counting either '3', '6', '9' ... or '4', '8', '12' ...).

<u>Key Idea</u>: People all over the earth need to learn about Jesus.

Dramatic Play

Use a globe or map to show where you live. Point out that people live all over the world. Have students pretend to be airplanes flying around the room. Have 1 student point to any place on the map or globe. Say, *We are landing in ____.* (Name the country the student pointed to.) Have the "planes" land and say, *Jesus died for you. Believe in him.* Repeat the game.

<u>Key Idea</u>: People from many different places heard about Jesus.

Corresponding Music

The Singing Bible, Disc 4 - Track 9
Song Title: *"Acts"*

Fingerplay: Zip, Zap, Zing

Days 1-5

Peter preaches.	*Hold arms out wide*
People believe.	*Bow head, fold hands*
Jesus saves them.	*Lift hands to heaven*
Zip! Zap! Zing!	*Snap fingers 3 times*

Peter and John pray.	*Fold hands*
The lame man pleads.	*Kneel*
Jesus heals him.	*Jump up*
Zip! Zap! Zing!	*Snap fingers 3 times*

Peter is in prison.	*Spread fingers over eyes*
The angel sets him free.	*Pull hands away from face*
Tell people about Jesus.	*Shake pointer finger*
Zip! Zap! Zing!	*Snap fingers 3 times*

The Spread of the Gospel

Fingerplay

Do the fingerplay *"Zip! Zap! Zing!"* Focus on the sound and motion for the letter 'Z'.

Key Idea: 'Z' = snap fingers and say *Z-Z*

Bible Story

Read the Bible story from **one** of the following resources:

✔ Scripture: Acts 3:6-10

✔ *The New Bible in Pictures for Little Eyes* p. 362-365

Key Idea: A lame man was healed.

Active Exploration

Students practice skipping and galloping. To practice skipping, have students hold a stuffed animal in front of their bodies and raise alternating knees to touch the animal as they skip. To practice galloping, students lead with one foot as the other foot lags behind in an uneven rhythm. For older students call out whether to skip or gallop, which foot to start with, and whether to go forward, to the side, or in a circle.

Key Idea: The man was healed. He leaped for joy and praised God.

Letter Activity

Write a big 'Z' on a piece of paper. Have students use fingerpaints, paints and paintbrushes, or playdough to fill in the letter.

Key Idea: Students will become familiar with the shape and appearance of the capital letter 'Z'.

Bible Activity

Act out the Bible story. Have the students pretend to be the lame man sitting on the ground by the gate. You pretend to be Peter. The lame man holds out his hands to you as if asking for money. Take the lame man by the hands and say, *In the name of Jesus you are healed. Get up and walk.* The lame man jumps up, and leaps, and skips through the room shouting, *Praise God! Praise God! Praise God!*

Key Idea: Peter healed the man in Jesus' name. The lame man gladly gave praise and thanks to the Lord for being healed.

Corresponding Music

The Singing Bible, Disc 4 - Track 9
Song Title: *"Acts"*

The Spread of the Gospel

Fingerplay

Do the fingerplay *"Zip! Zap! Zing!"* Focus on the sound and motion for the letter 'Z'.

<u>Key Idea</u>: 'Z' = snap fingers and say *Z-Z*

Bible Story

Read the Bible story from **one** of the following resources:

✔ Scripture: Acts 12:6-11

✔ *A Child's First Bible* p. 244-245

✔ *The New Bible in Pictures for Little Eyes* p. 368-369

<u>Key Idea</u>: God sent an angel to free Peter.

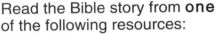

Art Activity

Give each student a piece of **yellow paper**. Cut strips of **aluminum foil**. Show students how to twist the aluminum foil into prison bars. Help students **tape** the bars to the yellow paper in vertical strips. The yellow is the angel's light shining through Peter's prison bars. Older students may draw Peter, cut him out, and glue him behind the prison bars.

<u>Key Idea</u>: Peter was set free from prison by God's angel.

Letter Activity

Use masking tape to make a large 'Z' on the floor. Have students place blocks on the tape to trace the letter. Each time a block is placed on the tape, students make the letter **sound**.

<u>Key Idea</u>: Each letter has a name and a sound, just like animals do. For example, a frog may be named Slimy, but it makes the sound, *Ribbit*.

Bible Activity

Act out the Bible story. The students are Peter sitting in jail with their wrists and ankles together to show his chains. You are the angel that taps Peter and tells him to get up and put on his cloak and sandels. Peter says, *The chains have fallen off.* Motion for Peter to follow you through the open prison door. Walk with Peter down the street and then disappear. Peter prays a prayer of thanks to the Lord.

<u>Key Idea</u>: Many people were praying for Peter, and God answered their prayers.

Corresponding Music

The Singing Bible, Disc 4 - Track 9
Song Title: *"Acts"*

The Spread of the Gospel

Fingerplay

Do the fingerplay *"Zip! Zap! Zing!"* Focus on the sound and motion for the letter 'Z'.

Key Idea: 'Z' = snap fingers and say *Z-Z*

Bible Story

Read the Bible story from **one** of the following resources:

✔ Scripture: Acts 6:8; 7:54-60
✔ *The New Bible in Pictures for Little Eyes* p. 370-371

Key Idea: Stephen went to be with Jesus in heaven.

Devotional Activity

Read and discuss the devotion from **one** of the following resources:

✔ *Big Thoughts for Little People*
Read the two pages for letter 'Z'.
✔ *Teach Them to Your Children*
Read the two pages for letter 'Z'.
✔ *My ABC Bible Verses*
Read the two pages for letter 'Z'.

Key Idea: Share a devotional focusing on character traits or memory work based on the letter 'Z'.

Letter Activity

Use the 'Z' flashcard from the Appendix. Have students trace the capital and small letter 'Z's' on the flashcard with their fingers. Using the flashcard as a model, choose either sidewalk chalk or 2 crayons taped together and paper to write more 'Z's'.

Key Idea: Practice the motions needed to make the letter 'Z'.

Bible Activity

Explain that missionaries go to other places or countries to tell others about Jesus. Talk about the missionaries your church supports or any other missionaries that you know. Explain that without missionaries many people in other places would never get the chance to know about Jesus, and they would never have a chance to go to heaven. Have the students practice telling one of their stuffed toys about Jesus. Prompt them as needed.

Key Idea: Missionaries go to other countries to tell people about Jesus.

Corresponding Music

The Singing Bible, Disc 4 - Track 17
Song Titles: *"Forever"*

The Spread of the Gospel

Fingerplay

Do the fingerplay *"Zip! Zap! Zing!"*
Focus on the sound and motion for the
letter 'Z'.

<u>Key Idea</u>: 'Z' = snap fingers and say
Z-Z

Bible Story

Read the Bible story from **one**
of the following resources:

✔ Scripture: Acts 8:26-31, 35

✔ *The New Bible in Pictures for
Little Eyes* p. 372-373

<u>Key Idea</u>: Philip did what God said.

Math Activity

<u>Youngers</u>: Practice dividing a graham
cracker into 2 equal parts. Show
students how to lay the halves on top
of each other to be sure they are equal.
Next, divide a square cracker. Last,
divide a circular cracker or snack.
<u>Olders</u>: Show students how to equally
divide a group of objects. Place the
objects in the center. Pass out one at
a time to each person, continuing until
the objects are gone. Count the
objects.

<u>Key Idea</u>: The man only had part of
the Bible, yet he understood that Jesus
died to save him.

Letter Activity

Copy the *Hide and Seek 'Z'* page.
Have students circle, color, highlight, or
point to the 'Z's' on the page. Younger
students may need help in order to find
any 'Z's' at all. It is not necessary to
find all the 'Z's'. On the bottom of the
page, have students connect 'Z' to 'z'
by tracing the dotted line from left to
right.

<u>Key Idea</u>: Students should eventually
recognize the capital and small letter
'Z' within words.

Bible Activity

Give each student a piece of paper.
Help students complete each of the
following directions one at a time:
Draw a black rectangle on the left side
of the page to be a Bible. Draw a
question mark on the right side of the
page. Draw a blue, wavy line on the
bottom of the page to be a river.

<u>Key Idea</u>: As the Ethiopian man was
reading the Bible, he had some
questions. Philip spoke to the man and
told him about Jesus. Then, the man
was baptized in the river.

Corresponding Music

The Singing Bible, Disc 4 - Track 17
Song Titles: *"Forever"*

Hide and Seek 'Z'

Peter preaches.

People believe.

Jesus saves them.

Zip! Zap! Zing!

Z ---------------------------------- Z

Z ---------------------------------- Z

The Apostle Paul

Fingerplay

Do the fingerplay *"What Do You Know?"* Focus on reviewing the sounds and motions for the letters.

Key Idea: Practice the sounds and motions for the letters 'A-Z'.

Bible Story

Read the Bible story from **one** of the following resources:

✔ Scripture: Acts 9:1-3

✔ *A Child's First Bible* p. 238

✔ *The New Bible in Pictures for Little Eyes* p. 374-375

Key Idea: Saul hurt Christians.

Art Activity

Give each student a sheet of **white paper**. Use a **permanent marker** to draw 4 dark lines on each paper like light shining from heaven. Have students **color** or **paint** each section between the lines a different color. If students use paint, they may fingerpaint or use brushes to paint each section.

Key Idea: As Saul was going to Damascus to capture Christians, a bright light from heaven stopped him.

Letter Activity

This is a review week. Review all the flashcards from the previous weeks. Show the letter side of each flashcard to the students. Have them respond with the motion and sound. If needed, read the *Hint* or demonstrate the motion and sound.

Key Idea: Students should eventually do the motion and say the sound for each flashcard without needing a *Hint* or a demonstration.

Bible Activity

Tell students to do the following actions: *Make a mad face. Use an angry voice to say, "I don't like you." Stomp around and shake your fists in the air.* Ask students, *How does it feel to be so angry? Does God want us to be angry and hurt others?* Tell students to do the following happy actions: *Smile. Use a happy voice and say, "I like you". Skip around and make a happy face. Clap your hands and laugh.* Ask students, *Did it feel better to be happy? Why?*

Key Idea: Saul didn't believe in Jesus. He hated Christians.

Corresponding Music

The Singing Bible, Disc 4 - Track 10
Song Title: *"The New Man Paul"*

Fingerplay: What Do You Know?

We've learned about *A-A-Adam*	*Hands on cheeks in surprise*
And *B-B-Boat,*	*Hug yourself and rock side-to-side*
C-C-Clippity clop	*Tap palms on thighs in rhythm*
And *D-D-Dusty* camel.	*Hold reins of camel and move*
	up-down-up-down
E-E-Empty jars	*Shake hand to shake empty jar*
And *F-F-Fire,*	*Wiggle 10 fingers like flames*
G-G-Gurgle	*Hold nose, put hand up*
And *H-H-Helping* hands.	*Lace fingers, move up and down*
I-Impossible	*Push palms up as if lifting*
And *J-J-Joyful* jumping,	*2 fingers jump on palm of hand*
K-K-clapping hands	*Clap hands above head*
And *L-L-La-La-La.*	*Swing hand back and forth*
M-M-Miracles	*Pat hand over mouth, pull it away*
And *N-N-Naughty* king,	*Tap top of hand with 2 fingers*
O-O-Off	*Brush one hand with the other*
And *P-P-Pulling* oars.	*Make fists and pull them in*
Q-Q-Quivering	*Shake whole body*
And *R-R-Ready* to choose,	*Hold chin with hand, thinking*
S-S-Storms blowing	*Cover ears*
And *T-Time* to move.	*Tap wrist with finger, jump up*

Fingerplay: What Do You Know?
(continued)

Days 1-5

U-U, Uh-Uh	*Shake head, "No"*
And *V-V-Voice,*	*Touch throat with hand*
W-Wipe sins away	*Make circular wiping motion*
And *X-X* marks the spot.	*Make 'X' with index fingers*
Y-Y-Yeah	*Punch fist in the air twice*
And *Z-Z-Zing.*	*Snap fingers 3 times*
Now, as Paul	
Hears Jesus is God's son,	*Cup hand to ear*
He changes his ways	*Make a path with hands*
So that Jesus' will is done.	*Point up*
Just like the others	*Open palms together like Bible*
God has plans for you too.	*Point up, then point to yourself*
Never forget	*Shake head, "No"*
What God can do!	*Spread arms wide*

The Apostle Paul

Fingerplay

Do the fingerplay *"What Do You Know?"* Focus on reviewing the sounds and motions for the letters.

<u>Key Idea</u>: Practice the sounds and motions for the letters 'A-Z'.

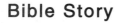
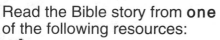

Bible Story

Read the Bible story from **one** of the following resources:

✔ Scripture: Acts 9:3-8

✔ *A Child's First Bible* p. 239

✔ *The New Bible in Pictures for Little Eyes* p. 376-377

<u>Key Idea</u>: Jesus spoke to Saul.

Active Exploration

Put a sticker on top of each student's right hand. Explain to students that the hands with the stickers are their right hands. The hands without stickers are their left hands. Have students get in line and walk behind you. Call out either, *left* or *right,* each time you come to a corner. Students follow your directions, checking their hands to make sure they are turning the appropriate way.

<u>Key Idea</u>: Now, Saul does what Jesus says. He is a new man, Paul.

Letter Activity

Choose one letter from 'A-Z' to review. Write that letter on a big piece of paper. Have students glue cotton balls or pieces of yarn to the letter. Younger students will need you to apply drops of glue on the letter for them first.

<u>Key Idea</u>: Students will become familiar with the shape and appearance of the capital letters.

Bible Activity

Act out the Bible story. Tell students to pretend to be Paul walking down the road to Damascus. Direct students to cover their eyes and kneel down on the ground. You be the voice of Jesus and say, *Saul, why do you persecute me? I am Jesus. Go to the city.* Have students get up and feel their way forward as if they are blind. Then, have students kneel in prayer and wait.

<u>Key Idea</u>: Saul did not know Jesus is God's Son. He believed after Jesus spoke to him and made him blind.

Corresponding Music

The Singing Bible, Disc 4 - Track 10
Song Title: *"The New Man Paul"*

The Apostle Paul

Fingerplay

Do the fingerplay *"What Do You Know?"* Focus on reviewing the sounds and motions for the letters.

Key Idea: Practice the sounds and motions for the letters 'A-Z'.

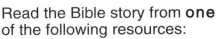

Bible Story

Read the Bible story from **one** of the following resources:

✔ Scripture: Acts 9:23-27

✔ *A Child's First Bible* p. 240-241

✔ *The New Bible in Pictures for Little Eyes* p. 378-379

Key Idea: Paul left in a basket.

Dramatic Play

Gather the following props: a brown paper rectangle or a basket, a grey paper square or a block, a yellow paper triangle or a folded napkin, a blue paper circle or a bowl with water. Scatter the props on the floor. Instruct students to tiptoe to the brown basket and crouch down, tiptoe to the blue circle of water and row, tiptoe to the triangle-shaped tent and lay down, and tiptoe around the square which is the city.

Key Idea: God watched over Paul and helped him get away.

Letter Activity

Copy the *Hide and Seek Review* page. Choose either 'Y' or 'Z' to review. Have students circle, color, highlight, or point to the chosen letter. Younger students may need help in order to find any of the chosen letters. On the bottom of the page, have students draw a line to connect each capital letter to its matching lowercase letter.

Key Idea: Students should eventually recognize the capital and small letters 'Y' and 'Z' within words.

Bible Activity

Copy *Count on Me* (in Appendix). Direct students to draw baskets by making brown ovals in each of the boxes. Younger students make 3 baskets in each box. Older students make 4 baskets in each box. Point to each basket as you count it. Write the numbers on the lines below each box as you count. Say the numbers below the boxes to count by 3's or by 4's (counting either '3', '6', '9' ... or '4', '8', '12' ...).

Key Idea: Paul's friends hid him in a basket to lower him over the wall.

Corresponding Music

The Singing Bible, Disc 4 - Track 10
Song Title: *"The New Man Paul"*

Hide and Seek Review

We've learned about Y-Y-Yeah

And Zip! Zap! Zing!

Never forget

Jesus is our king.

Z

z

Y

y

Z

z

Y

y

The Apostle Paul

Fingerplay

Do the fingerplay *"What Do You Know?"* Focus on reviewing the sounds and motions for the letters.

Key Idea: Practice the sounds and motions for the letters 'A-Z'.

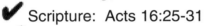

Bible Story

Read the Bible story from **one** of the following resources:

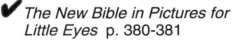 Scripture: Acts 16:25-31

✔ *A Child's First Bible* p. 250-251

✔ *The New Bible in Pictures for Little Eyes* p. 380-381

Key Idea: Paul and Silas were in prison.

Math Activity

Gather 10 blocks with various colors, sizes, and shapes. Have students put the blocks in a bucket or towel, shake them as if there is an earthquake, and dump them in a pile on the floor. Tell students the following things to do: Sort the blocks by color, then by shape, and last by size. Older students may sort more blocks with more colors, shapes, or sizes.

Key Idea: God sent the earthquake to free Paul and Silas from jail.

Letter Activity

Choose one or more of the letters 'A-Z' to review. Use masking tape to make the large review letter on the floor. Have students drive a toy car or other toy vehicle on the tape to trace the letter. Have students say the letter **sound** as they drive.

Key Idea: Each letter has a name and a sound, just like animals do. For example, a lion may be named Leo, but it makes the sound, *Roar.*

Bible Activity

Give each student a piece of paper. Help students complete each of the following directions one at a time: Draw 3 black lines at the top of the page to be prison bars. Draw a red smile on the left side of the page to be the men singing. Draw a brown 't' on the right side of the page to be a cross.

Key Idea: Paul and Silas were in prison singing praises to the Lord. The earth shook, and the prison doors were opened. The guard asked about Jesus and believed.

Corresponding Music

The Singing Bible, Disc 4-Track 11, 17
Song Titles: *"Send it in a Letter"*
"Forever"

The Apostle Paul

Fingerplay

Do the fingerplay *"What Do You Know?"* Focus on reviewing the sounds and motions for the letters.

Key Idea: Practice the sounds and motions for the letters 'A-Z'.

Bible Story

Read the Bible story from **one** of the following resources:

✔ Scripture: Acts 27:22-26

✔ *The New Bible in Pictures for Little Eyes* p. 382-383

Key Idea: God saved Paul from the storm.

Devotional Activity

Read and discuss the devotion from **one** of the following resources:

✔ *Big Thoughts for Little People*
Review verses for 'Y' and 'Z'

✔ *Teach Them to Your Children*
Review verses for 'Y' and 'Z'

My ABC Bible Verses
Review verses for 'Y' and 'Z'

Key Idea: Share a devotional focusing on character traits or memory work based on the letters 'Y' and 'Z'.

Letter Activity

Choose one or more of the flashcards from the previous weeks to review. Have students trace the capital and small letters on the flashcards with their fingers. Using the flashcards as models, give students either a small amount of cooking oil or liquid soap on an aluminum pan or plate to practice writing more letters.

Key Idea: Practice the motions needed to make the letters.

Bible Activity

Act out the Bible story. Give students the following directions: *Make a sound like the wind. Stand up and rock back and forth. Pretend to jump into the water. Lay down and pretend to swim. Stand up and make climbing motions. Kneel down and pray. Say, "Thank you Lord".*

Key Idea: God saved Paul and everyone on the boat from the storm.

Corresponding Music

The Singing Bible, Disc 4-Track 11, 17
Song Titles: *"Send it in a Letter"*
"Forever"

Books by This Author:

Little Hands to Heaven
A preschool program for ages 2-5

Little Hearts for His Glory
An early learning program for ages 5-7

Beyond Little Hearts for His Glory
An early learning program for ages 6-8

Bigger Hearts for His Glory
A learning program for ages 7-9
With extensions for ages 10-11

Preparing Hearts for His Glory
A learning program for ages 8-10
With extensions for ages 11-12

Hearts for Him Through Time: Creation to Christ
A learning program for ages 9-11
With extensions for ages 12-13

Hearts for Him Through Time: Resurrection to Reformation
A learning program for ages 10-12
With extensions for ages 13-14

Drawn into the Heart of Reading
A literature program for ages 7-15 that
Works with any books you choose

These books are published by
Heart of Dakota Publishing, Inc.

See the website: www.heartofdakota.com
For placement information, product details, or to order a catalog

For ordering questions, email: carmikeaustin@msn.com
Or, call: 605-428-4068